THE ORDER OF THE S.S.

THE ORDER OF THE S.S.

by Frederic Reider

AZTEX Corporation, Tucson, AZ

ISBN 0-89404-061-8

Library of Congress Catalog Card No. 81-52162
© English translation and Introduction.
W. Foulsham & Co. Ltd
Yeovil Road, Slough, Berks, England
Originally published in the French language as
L'Ordre S.S. by Éditions de la Pensée Moderne © 1975.

All rights reserved. No part of this book may be reproduced or transmitted in any form or by any means, electronic or mechanical, including photocopying, recording or by any information storage or retrieval system, without permission in writing from the publisher.

Typeset by Computacomp (UK) Ltd,
Fort William, Scotland
Printed in Hong Kong

AZTEX Corporation
PO Box 50046, Tucson, AZ 85703

CONTENTS

Introduction	Germany and the Causes and Consequences of the First World War................	7
Chapter 1.	The Anger of the Young Infantrymen. Germany in Distress – the Origins of Nazism (1919–1923).......................	15
Chapter 2.	Your Honour is Your Loyalty. Birth of the S.S. (1924–1932)....................	39
Chapter 3.	The New Inquisition. Taking Power and the Security Service (1932–1937)...........	65
Chapter 4.	The Empire of the Black Prince. The Tentacles of the S.S...................	95
Chapter 5.	The Blood Myth. Ideology in the Form of a Religion.......................	128
Chapter 6.	The Reichsfuhrer's Cadets. The Napolas – Schools for Future Leaders of the Third Reich.........................	157
Chapter 7.	The Secret Laboratory of the Millenary Reich. The Ahnenerbe, the S.S. University.......	185
Chapter 8.	The Black Order. Himmler Speaks........	205
Index	....	254

Appendices

I.	Badges of rank of the Allgemeine S.S. (1934)......	228
II.	Badges and decorations of the Allgemeine S.S. and the Waffen S.S............................	231
III.	Special badges of the Allgemeine S.S............	236
IV.	Armbands..............................	239
V.	Territorial organisation of the S.S. (1943).........	241
VI.	Main events in the history of the S.S.	243
VII.	Structure of the S.S.	249

The Publishers believed that this book would be made more useful if an introduction setting out the general context in which events in Germany unfolded after 1918 were added. They therefore asked Richard Langhorne, Fellow of St. John's College, Cambridge to write a brief introductory chapter. He is the author of several articles on Anglo-German relations before the First World War and of a book on international politics in general 1890–1914: *The Collapse of the Concert of Europe*, (Macmillan, 1981).

Introduction

Germany and the Causes and Consequences of the First World War

The whole of Europe was disrupted to some extent by the consequences of the First World War and the ensuing settlement. For some societies, disruption was mainly economic, but for others, particularly perhaps in central Europe, the most dramatic effects seemed to be territorial and political. For all of Europe, the psychological consequences of the casualties on every side, and the onset of the Russian revolution, created marked anxieties about future stability, about the maintenance of peace and even about the continuation of European civilisation.

In Germany, all these effects were to be seen rendered even more compelling by the particular circumstances of defeat. They are well documented and have been widely discussed, often as part of the explanations for the eventual success of Hitler. For Germany, naturally, the principal additional difficulty arose from the way in which the war ended. It had amounted to an effective defeat. Despite the formal armistice of November 1918, which implied a negotiated end to the war, Germany was thereafter treated by the allies as a defeated party. Even the basis upon which the armistice had been agreed – President Wilson's 14 points – was abandoned, and the new German government, the existence of which was itself a precondition for peace, was excluded from the subsequent peace conference held at Paris in 1919. In the end a new regime in Germany which, in 1918, was widely believed to have "stabbed the armed forces in the back", was compelled to sign a peace treaty with which it did not comply, and yet to become, practically speaking, the only agency by which the conditions of peace could be fulfilled. Those conditions had three aspects which were particularly galling to Germany. The first was that the principle of national self-determination was operated against Germans, both in border realignments and, above all, in the creation of German Austria as a separate state. Secondly, the treaty imposed compensatory payments upon Germany, which were believed by some economists to be unpayable, and by many others to be morally wrong, since they depended upon the unprovable assertion, made in Article 231 of the Treaty, that Germany was guilty for the war. Thirdly, the Treaty imposed disarmament upon all powers, but began by actually disarming Germany and leaving the disarmament of others to follow. It was always unlikely that disarmament would succeed and, as time went on, it became quite apparent that it only applied to Germany.

In Europe, much disrupted and confused by the effects of the war, it gradually became obvious that there was no counter force available which was sufficiently strong to insist upon the terms of peace being obeyed by Germany. Indeed, there grew up the conviction that the settlement would have to be re-negotiated gradually, and that an eventual domination of post-war Europe by Germany would have to be controlled by bringing her back into the comity of states. In these circumstances, it was not surprising that ambitions which had been behind German policy before the First World War should reappear, even perhaps in a more extreme form.

Europe before the First World War

The historical literature about pre-war Europe and about the diplomacy of the Great Powers during this period is vast. It has been possible, however, to identify certain stages. At first, historians concentrated upon trying to prove whether or not Germany had been, as was stated in the Treaty, guilty for The War. The result was a great concentration upon the final crisis of 1914, and the publication of huge collections of diplomatic documents. When this seemed to produce only the conclusion that all powers were equally to blame for The War, historians began to take a wider view – after the Second World War had intervened to put 1914 into great perspective. If it was agreed that powers had seemed to slip unwillingly into war in 1914, the question arose as to how an international situation had arisen in which the War could occur. In this context, discussions of the great changes in the characteristics and behaviour of states during the last quarter of the nineteenth century became important. So also did assessments of the equally great changes in the scope of international politics, as more effective communications made the world into a single international stage.

This was a world in which it became possible to explain much by reference to shifts in the distribution of power away from Europe, shifts especially seen during the Far Eastern crises of 1895–1905. Yet, these shifts were to some extent concealed by the rapid rise of Germany to European domination. Europe seemed to possess all the attributes of power, and Germany seemed to be prepared to use this fact (and her own dominant position) to expand, and thus to defend herself, and perhaps Europe as a whole. This consideration has led to the most recent phase in the historical literature of the period.

New research carried out on German records seemed to show clearly that, quite separately from German policy during the 1914 crisis, there was evidence that German leaders over a considerable period had come to form positive long-term international plans arising out of their felt need to react to both an external and an internal threat. The external threat was seen principally as coming from the rise of Russia, whose political disturbances did not conceal, from the Germans at least, that she was going through a period of economic growth which has not yet been exceeded by any other country. This provided a temptation – in some eyes a necessity – to intervene by some means or other, most probably war, in order that Germany should use her domination of Europe to achieve genuine world power status.

This wide ambition was fuelled also at a narrower level of strategic discussion by the fact that Germany's rise in Europe, coupled with her efforts to claim a world position after 1897, had generated an anxious coalition of somewhat ill-assorted partners against her, and led to the practical defection of one of her allies, Italy. The alliance of Britain, France and Russia, which was completed with the Anglo-Russian agreement of 1907, was not intended to be aggressive. But for Germany it represented a deliberate encirclement and induced in her a strong desire to break out of the ring.

Power of the German Government increases

These developments produced at once a strong national sense of power and opportunity, and a strong sense of danger. The discussion of Germany's position was minute and persistent, for it was very much the age of academic geo-politics. The assertions and anxieties of German professors spilt over into newspapers and journals. The tone of debates in the German parliament was affected by it, as it was also by another preoccupation of the time: namely the cycle of rise and decay created by struggles leading to the survival of the fittest amongst nations provided a justification and an explanation for vigorous policies. The great vigour and economic and technological success of Wilhelmine Germany could be seen as giving her the right and duty to seize what she needed from the decaying powers – of which Britain and France were the obvious examples. Frustration caused by what could so easily be seen as useless opposition to the inevitable rise of Germany came to be a deeply seated view particularly among the German middle classes.

It was more likely that this kind of forward foreign policy would be pursued if, in addition to the external temptations already discussed, there were internal tensions which might make German governments seek relief in external adventures. All the great European states experienced an increase of internal tensions during the last quarter of the nineteenth century. They arose from major changes in economic and social structures which were caused by rapid industrial and technological advances. In particular, these changes, together with a population explosion (most marked in Germany) gave a much greater role to the state. Governments found themselves both able and expected to undertake a far greater range of activities than ever before.

The economic and social changes which came in the wake of a technologically based industrial revolution, occurring at high speed, naturally produced grave problems of adjustment. But more than that, they produced demands for change which threatened the basis upon which national Germany had been brought into existence. National Germany had been designed to buttress the traditionalist political and social position of Prussia. The institutions of the second Reich were also meant to serve that end. The domination of the agrarian groups of the north east, supported by the bourgeoisie of the south and west, was not compatible with the development of huge conurbations, great manufacturing companies and industrial and commercial magnates. Nor were the political consequences permissible. The growth of the Socialist party, though hampered as much as possible, continued steadily until by the turn of the century it had become the greatest Socialist party in Europe. The development of trade unions, too, was a threatening element in the eyes of traditionalist Germany. There was no doubt that the social mould of Germany had been radically changed, and that the political consequences posed a most serious threat to the dearest ideals and ambitions of the Prussian-German tradition. The German middle class which, in the face of the demands of the Socialists, had become almost fervent admirers of the Prussian element in the German idea, was the first great middle class in Europe to feel afraid. It is not surprising to discover that the course of German politics from the 1880s onward was dominated by the struggle of the élite to retain the power they had acquired after 1871.

To do so, they used as their weapon the fear of foreign activities; they tried to meet some of the demands for social reform half way in order to slow the political advance of the reformers; and they manipulated the machinery of government so as to retain control over the levers of power. This last enabled them to offer a shady alliance to the great industrialists, who would shun public political power in favour of private political influence, and they successfully offered the bait of social stability to a frightened middle class, who in return made little attempt to emulate the rise to political power of their equivalents in other European societies undergoing similar struggles.

Social Upheavals in Pre-war Germany

In the end, the failure of the constitutional system to respond to structural change in Germany society became too obvious. Neither political disguises, nor the glories of a grand external policy, nor the creation of the High Seas Fleet, nor the allure of the Crown (particularly not under the quixotic management of William II), proved to be able to preserve Germany from unmanageable social and political tension. Indeed, in 1908–9 and again in 1912, tension dipped at times into actual disorder and, as had happened in 1897, talk of a coup d'état began to be commonplace. This time, however, there was also some feeling that the advances of the Socialist party and the trade unions had made them too strong to be purged by a coup d'état. Only a preventive war might now do what no internal manipulation could do: that was to bring about the reunification of German society under the Crown.

Towards the end, a highly dramatic contrast developed between the visible economic and military might of Germany and her growingly depressed sense that she was under mortal threat. The threat was both internal – to the moral, social and institutional order; and external – to the security of the Reich, both in its European position and in its long-term ambitions in the world. The advent of mass politics had had its most profound effect in Germany where, because the constitutional machinery had been weakened, political propaganda began to be almost more important than political activity. Certainly the defenders of the *status quo* thought in such terms. Just before The War social rigidity, too, produced some striking contradictions. For example, despite the sense that Germany's military predominance was coming under threat from new measures taken in Russia and France, there was a reluctance to increase the size of the army, because it would have meant admitting politically unreliable workers to the ordinary ranks (who would have to be "re-educated") and of commissioning officers from outside the ruling élite.

The War of 1914 was not solely the result of considerations such as these. But it was the result of German desperation working on an international situation which presented both an opportunity and a threat: the one suggested the need for a preventive war, the other provided the means and excuse for bringing it about. The result of The War, since it proved not to have been conclusive, produced no fundamental change, only damaging modifications in the pre-1914 situation. Tendencies that already existed were emphasised rather than altered or suppressed, and for Germany that proved to be true both internally and externally.

Richard Langhorne

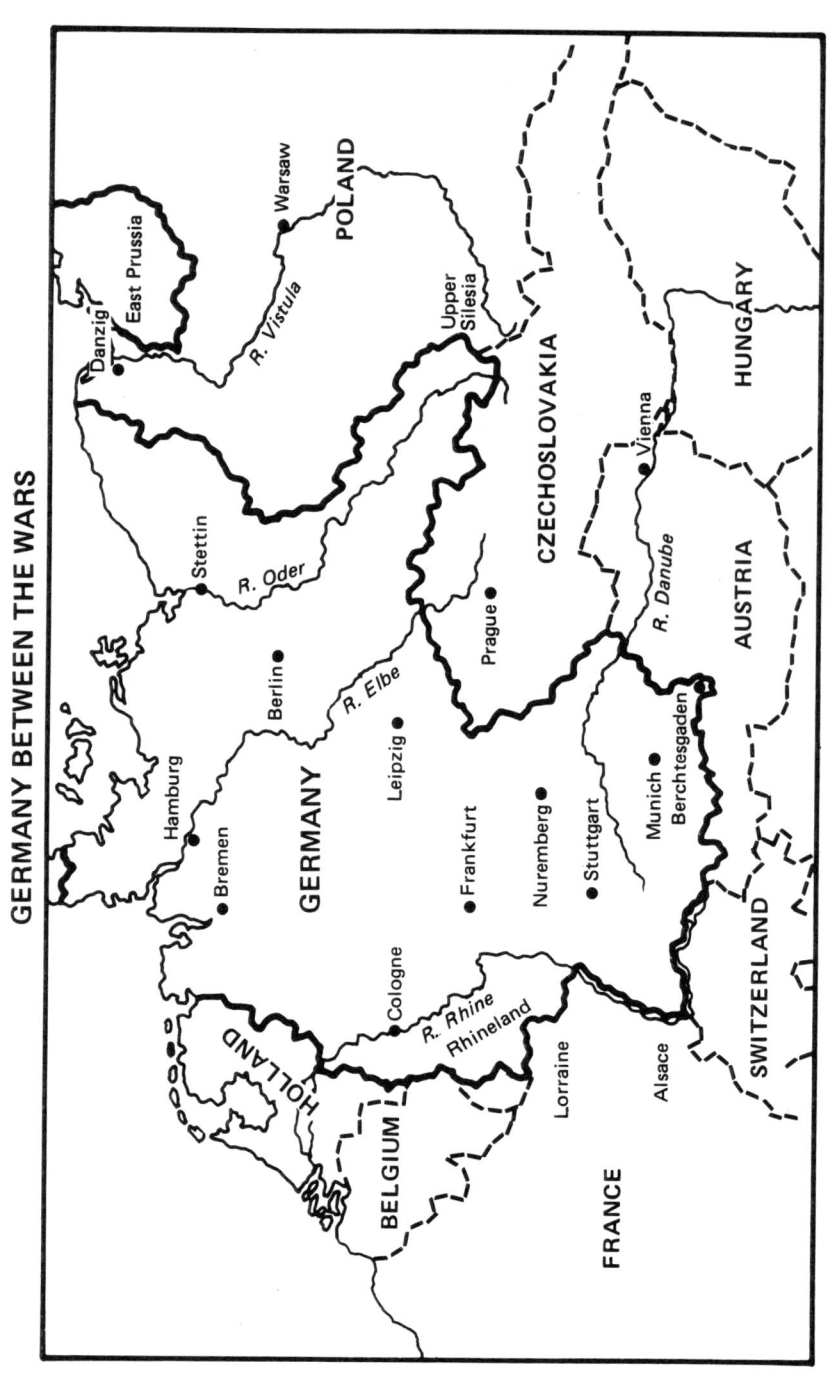

TERRITORY GAINED BY GERMANY IN 1938

The *Baltikum* Volunteer Corps was the forerunner of the Nazi organisation; it adopted the swastika as early as 1919. We see here men of the *Ehrhardt* Brigade.

CHAPTER 1

The Anger of the Young Infantrymen

Germany in Distress – the Origins of Nazism (1919–1923)

The date was 30th January 1933. Berlin resounded with shouts of triumph and the clatter of boots. When night spread over the capital – the first night of the Third Reich, the S.A. cohorts invaded the streets. Carrying torches held high above their heads, the brown tide swept under the Brandenburger Tor to salute its Führer, the former war-time corporal, now Chancellor of the Reich, called to this office by the will of the electors and the old President Hindenburg. Everywhere rang out the warcry of the National Socialists: *Deutschland Erwache!* (Germany Awake!)

Suddenly, the cries were stifled and the songs were interrupted. The crowd seemed to be holding its breath. In the chill silence was heard the thud of boots, growing louder with every second. In its funereal uniform, the S.S. took possession of the night. Not a smile lit up the impassive faces of the men in black. From the illuminated window of the Chancellery, Adolf Hitler gazed sternly on his élite pretorian guard, the messengers of a new world.

The S.S. was born out of chaos and the dreadful distress into which Germany was plunged at the end of the First World War.

"When I was treated as a convict, I thought I had reached the depths of human degradation and wretchedness," wrote Jean des Vallières, a French officer who was a prisoner of war at the disciplinary

In the Germany of 1919, those who had yesterday been heroes were reduced to misery and the worst humiliations (*Snark International*).

camp of Magdeburg in 1918.[1] "But worse was to come. There were the fearful ghost-like faces of children tortured by hunger. There were tragic skeletal women, squatting on the thresholds of their homes and gazing distractedly at the babies dying in their arms. One might have thought this was just a gallery of nightmares, a collection of unfortunate individuals. It was not so. This commercial quarter of the town was indeed just becoming one of the most active. These were whole families, who yesterday had been quite well off: shopkeepers, civil servants; the lower orders of the German middle class were enduring in pathetic silence, like slaves, a suffering worthy of hell."

The revolution broke out just behind the front, at Kiel, on 8th November 1918, with the assassination of two officers of the battleship, *König* – Captain Bruno Heinemann and Lieutenant-Commander Wolfgang Zenker. That same day, after fifty-one months of war, the Reich was forced to beg for an armistice from the Allies. Mutinies and uprisings became prevalent throughout Germany. The Kaiser abdicated on 9th November. A government of "Commissars of the People" was set up and the Republic proclaimed. In Berlin, the Spartacist riot threatened to rob the new regime of its legality.

[1] *Spartacus Parade* (Ed. Albin-Michel, 1932).

In a few days, the impressive apparatus of the Prussian State and the Imperial Army was completely dismantled.

Combatants returning from the front were welcomed by being spat upon. Their insignia were pulled from their uniforms. Officers who protested or defended themselves were attacked, and some were assassinated. In the town of Halle, dominated by the Red revolution, the armed crowd seized Lieutenant-Colonel von Klüwer. They beat him with their fists and their rifle butts. He fell to the ground. A kick broke his jaw and another stove in his ribs. They threw him in the River Saale. When the body came to the surface, it was greeted by howls of sadistic joy. The unfortunate officer tried to swim away in spite of his wounds, but the crowd threw stones at him from the bank. When he drew near the bank, almost breathless, they drummed on his fingers with their heels to make him let go and kicked him off. His bloody head was pushed under the water. This horrible game was interrupted by a Communist militiaman who finished him off with a pistol shot. Everywhere, from Bavaria to the Baltic ports, these scenes were common.

The revolution broke out just behind the front in November 1918. This bitter memory was later to foment the myth of the "stab in the back".

Recruiting posters for a volunteer corps in 1919.

The conditions laid down by the Armistice required that the German forces be rapidly withdrawn. Still disciplined as long as they were in contact with the enemy, in the trenches of Flanders or along the Aisne and the Somme, the troops were disbanded as soon as they returned to Germany. Most of the soldiers thought only of getting rid of their uniforms and, forgetting the mud, the vermin and the terror of the trenches, falling into the arms of a woman or sinking into the warmth of a home. They were hungry for some gentleness and rest. However,

The *Baltikum* Volunteer Corps; it prepared the way for the nihilistic revolution.

Germany — broken, ruined, hungry, as she was — was not able to give them this. Instead, they found duty-dodgers who had grown fat and were installed in the best positions, whereas they, hungry and tired, had to beg their living from door to door, in their threadbare uniforms. They saw wealth, pleasure and well-being reserved for the profiteers of the War, for which they had paid with their physical suffering.

It was out of this chaos and misery that the first volunteer corps organisations arose spontaneously. It needed only some young officer or non-commissioned officer to be goaded by his comrades in a maddened barracks to stand up on a table and call for volunteers to surround him. Those who answered the call were sickened by defeat and the disorganisation all around them. They had too much youth on their side; they were too full of energy to tolerate insults without answering them. They could not recognise themselves in the face of the new Germany.

Demagogues, dishevelled agitators and corrupt dealers, who were now at the top of the tree, inspired them with nothing but anger and contempt. Such men had often not even known the War; instead, they had conducted their sly operations behind the front. Paradoxically, the volunteer corps were shortly to become for a time the defenders of the politicians whom they abhorred. Ebert's socialist government was threatened by Spartacist revolution. Germany was on the point of meeting the same fate as Russia. The mayor of Cologne, one Konrad Adenauer, gravely confided to a journalist on *Le Matin* on 16th January 1919: "There isn't an army any more. Germany is in grave danger of falling to Bolshevism." The Government appealed to the volunteer corps to defend it. The new Minister of Defence, Noske, encouraged the formation of new volunteer corps. He was later to depend upon

Armoured car of the volunteer corps which re-conquered Munich on 2nd May 1919. The Death's Head, to be taken over later by the S.S., was depicted on the vehicle as a challenge both to the Red revolution and to the bourgeois Weimar Republic.

them, in 1919, to crush the spartacist insurrections at Berlin, and then later in the northern ports, the Ruhr and Bavaria.

Away in the East, in the *Baltikum* (Baltic countries), other volunteer corps members were to fight throughout 1919 to build up a new German fatherland. Abandoned and rejected by their own government, they in turn strove to promote the revolution of nihilism. They chose as their emblem the Death's Head, the traditional insignia of the élite regiments of the Prussian cavalry, as the dreadful symbol of their defiance.

The name of *Baltikum* became the symbol of the volunteer corps which arose throughout Germany, born of defeat and civil war. First used, and then rejected, by the Weimar Republic, which feared them, they took part in the Kapp Putsch, the fighting in Silesia, the assassination of Rathenau, the resistance movement in the Ruhr and the skirmish of the Black Reichswehr.

They had leaders, *Führers*, whom they had chosen, and they recognised none but these. Pitiless and contemptuous, they were moved by an indescribable passion. They rose up on the huge dislocated body of the Reich, driven forward by the terrifying force of their youth and despair.

Their deathly and bloody standards cracked in the wind like a wild challenge thrown at the ruins of the old world and the strange prophets of universal chaos.[1]

Like Ernst von Salomon, they said: "We didn't want what we knew, and we didn't know what we wanted."

A stranger on the scene was to formulate with clarity what they felt only confusedly. This was Adolf Hitler. He was a lean, hard, wolf-like man. He made his public debut in 1919 at Munich, before a group of the national resistance against the Weimar Republic and Communism. It was there that the former volunteer corps members took refuge after their disbandment throughout Germany.

From the age of 15, Hitler had sensed his vocation as a tribune of the people and as a revolutionary. He was a rebel, revolting against his father, his teachers and the decadent Austria of the Habsburgs. He already felt himself to be a German nationalist. He discovered in Vienna how hard it was to have to fight for existence. His trade as a commercial painter did not bring him in enough to eat. He had to visit the soup

---

[1] See Dominique Venner, *Baltikum* (Ed. Laffont, 1974).

Lieutenant Erwin Kern, the assassin of the government minister Rathenau. A calculated fanatic, he was driven with the terrifying power of youth and despair.

Adolf Hitler in 1920. He was a lean and hard, wolf-like man, fashioned in war.

kitchens and had to work as a labourer on building sites. His anti-semitism, his hatred of the Marxists whom he saw at work and his ideas about propaganda and political action grew out of these difficult years. The world conflict was to leave an indelible mark on this Bohemian character.

The horror of the battlefield made him not a pacifist, but a man devoid of pity. Just as the volunteer corps had, he might well have thought of the words of Ernst Jünger: "War is our mother; she has forged us, modelled us, hardened us and made us what we are. As long as the wheel of pulsing life drives us on, war will be the axle around which it will turn."

In November 1918, Corporal Hitler, who had the distinction, rare for a member of the rank-and-file, to be decorated with the Iron Cross, First Class, found himself in hospital. He had been gassed on the front and had temporarily lost his sight. While he was there he heard, in succession, about the revolution in Berlin, the abdication of the Kaiser and the defeat. "The days, and even more the nights that came after them," he was to write in *Mein Kampf*, "were horrible. I knew that everything was lost. In these sleepless nights, I felt growing in me the hatred of those who had been responsible for this disaster. It was then that I learnt of my true destiny. I took the decision to become a man of politics."

Following on the break-up of the Soviet Republic in Bavaria, in 1919, the Bavarian Volunteer Corps organised a propaganda service to get control of the units which had been infiltrated in part by the Communists. Corporal Hitler was enrolled for this job. He quickly made his mark by his natural oratorical gifts, and was appointed *Bildungsoffizier*, responsible for psychological training.

Throughout the first few days of September 1919, his superior, Captain Mayr, asked him to keep his eye on the German Workers' Party, the *Deutsche Arbeiterpartei* (D.A.P.), with a view to taking advantage of this small patriotic association. It was a grouping which had been set up by the society known as *Thule*, bringing together racist intellectuals to fight Marxist influence and "Jewish infiltration" into the working class. This small group of men was presided over at Munich by a genuine worker, the mechanic Anton Drexler, but it was the

The Bavarian Volunteer Corps of General Ritter von Epp brings down the "Soviet Republic", set up at Munich in 1919.

intellectuals of *Thule* who pulled the strings – the journalist, Karl Harrer, the writer, Dietrich Eckart, the economist, Gottfried Feder and Dr. Friedrich Krohn.

Hitler attended a meeting of the D.A.P. on 12th September, as observer, along with forty-six other people, in the back room of the Sterneckbräu public house at Munich. He was dozing away peacefully, when suddenly one of those present got up to advocate vehemently that Bavaria be separated from the Reich; this was a popular theme in conservative Bavarian circles. Hitler jumped to his feet. In a passionate voice, he shattered the separatist's arguments and won the meeting over. As they went out, Drexler gave him a little brochure and invited him to a meeting of the management committee.

"Ghastly, absolutely ghastly," he was to note down in *Mein Kampf*. "A lowdown, backward party – the worst sort. Ought I really to join a party like that? After debating within myself for two days, and after much painful reflection, I ended by persuading myself that I had to take

The start of a political commitment with unpredictable consequences. Hitler receives on 1st January 1920 the membership card of the D.A.P., the future N.S.D.A.P., number 555.

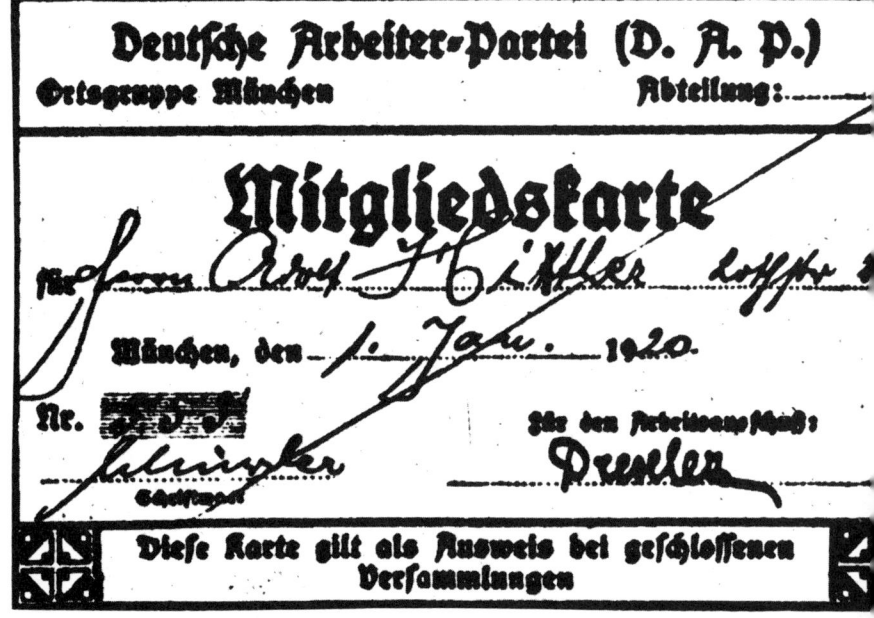

the plunge. This was the most momentous decision I ever took. There could be no return, nor should there be. I, therefore, agreed to become a member of the German Workers' Party." He was thirty at the time.

The man who had lost his class had become a fanatical revolutionary. "He detested the bourgeois order with the whole of his being. If he did come to any terms with it, it would be for the sole purpose of destroying it. He judged the former aristocracy, the heights of industry and the officer caste as irreconcilable adversaries. But he by no means adhered to any egalitarian belief; his socialism was Prussian, a military socialism, founded as much in his blood as in his readings. Moreover, his nationalism was not only that of a man who came from the fringes of the country; Germany, for him, was a way of living, feeling and behaving. His nationalist passion was reinforced by the attacks on *Deutschtum* (the German spirit), inflicted by foreign manners and ethics, which were of a nature to mortify him every day. He was a young man in suffering. The spectacle which had been offered him by Austria before 1914 and Germany since 1918 flayed him alive. In this torment of soul, he was to generate the fires which would later kindle the universe.[1]

His hatred of the Reds and his anti-semitism fed on the spectacle presented by Germany in these troubled years. He never ceased to confront the same adversaries as had the combatants of the volunteer corps. He found the Jews principally responsible for popular corruption. They were indeed the leaders of the leftist movement: Landsberg, Hasse, Liebknecht and Rosa Luxemburg at Berlin; Kurt Eisner, Lipp, Landauer Toller, Levine and Lewien at Munich; Brandes at Magdeburg; Lipinsky, Geyer and Fleissner at Dresden; Makus and Levinsohn in the Ruhr; Grünewald and Kohn in the North Sea ports; Lilienthal and Heine in the Palatinate and Ulmanis in Lithuania. "Give me a name, and I will show you a Jew," said Benoist-Mechin.[2] "When the parties of the Left decided to set up a commission of enquiry and make Hindenburg and Ludendorff appear before it, who were the inspirers of that idea? Messrs. Kohn, Gothein and Zinsheimer – and the list could be infinitely prolonged. How was it possible not to see in this a real conspiracy?"

---

[1] See Dominique Venner, *op. cit.*

[2] *History of the German Army* (Ed. Albin-Michel) Vol. II.

Before Hitler, the swastika was the emblem of nationalist and anti-semitic movements and societies, like the *Thule* Society.

It was from this belief that Hitler drew his Manichaean ideas of a Germanic race, which was endowed with all virtues and all creative capacities, facing a parasitic and destructive Jewish people. His task was clear – to liberate the German people from what he regarded as a noxious germ. This ambition was to find a loud echo in the ranks of the volunteer corps.

These bodies provided the young *Bildungsoffizier* with his first partisans. Their recruitment was made in agreement with his superiors, Captain Mayr and especially Captain Röhm, the adjutant of General Ritter von Epp, head of the volunteer corps which had liberated Munich. A bold warrior and a man of the infantry with a strong political sense, a lover of derring-do and a great schnaps drinker, Röhm lived feverishly in anticipation of a nationalist revolution of a military type which would divide the liberal bourgeois and the Communists. He

A nationalist engraving from the beginning of the century. Its caption reads: "A vision of the future". Germany, represented by the Emperor and the Army, is confronting Jewry, spivs, Socialists and rabbis, all appearing together (*Federal Archives, Koblenz*).

rapidly summed up the exceptional gifts of his *Bildungsoffizier*, Hitler, sending to him an incessant flood of officers, non-commissioned officers and privates, members of self-defence militias such as the *Orgesch* or those who had served in volunteer corps. Thus, in October 1920, the veterans of the Iron Division of the *Baltikum* went over "en bloc" to the young party.

So far, Hitler had been an agent of the volunteer corps and the Army. He did not gain complete independence until after the Kapp Putsch. On 31st March 1920, he was released from Army control. To underline the changes brought about by this freedom of action, he changed the name of his party to *Nazional-Sozialistische Deutsche Arbeiter Partei* (N.S.D.A.P.) (the National Socialist German Worker Party).

The military nature of the Party grew with the setting-up of the infamous S.A. (*Sturmabteilung*) during 1921. This was the work of

The veterans of the Bavarian Volunteer Corps, disbanded by the Weimar Republic, bring Hitler his first supporters.

Captain Röhm, that great organiser of clandestine armed units in Bavaria. He used his protégé's Party to camouflage these operations, and Hitler was not difficult to convince. Some of the volunteer corps leaders, especially the well-known Captain Ehrhardt, were hostile to this politicisation, which they considered excessive, but others threw themselves headlong in support.

These outcasts brought along with them most of the myths, rites and symbols which were ultimately associated with the name of Hitler and his Party.

The designation "National Socialist" had existed since the end of the 19th Century among pan-Germanic groups in Sudetenland and Austria. The qualifying adjective *völkisch* was in use extensively among the members of the volunteer corps. The swastika served anti-semitic groupings as an emblem before 1914. A number of volunteer corps, including the Ehrhardt Brigade, had adopted it even before Hitler took it over. Anti-semitism, which was already a live issue before the War, was found extensively among the volunteer corps due to the presence of many Jews among the leaders of the Socialist and Spartacist Revolution. As for the Führer principle, this had been vigorously upheld within the youth movement before 1914, and the well-known *Stosstruppen* (Assault Troops) had surrounded it with honour during the War. The

Lieutenant Gerhard Rossbach, one of the most famous leaders of the volunteer corps, who was to invent the S.A.'s brown shirt; he was to become one of the organisers of the S.A.

slogan *Ein Reich, Ein Volk* (One Germany, One People) belonged to the pan-Germanic arsenal from before the War. Hitler added to it *Ein Führer* (One Leader). The designations used within the Party – *Sturmabteilung* (S.A. – Storm Troop), *Gau* (Region), *Kreiss* (County), *Abschnitt* (District), used by the S.A., and later by the S.S. – were copied from the Rossbach *Freikorps* (Volunteer Corps). It was, above all, Lieutenant Rossbach, a dominant figure at this time, who was to invent the brown shirt and force the S.A. to wear it. As an insult to his Socialist and Communist adversaries, Hitler borrowed from them the colour red for his flags, his armbands, his posters and his decors. He also used the example they had set to organise massive demonstrations – showing them, at the same time, how to organise them properly.

As Dominique Venner has pointed out[1]: "All the basic elements of Nazism were already there, although in dispersion, when Hitler made his appearance on the scene. He did not need to invent them. He only drew them together to make out of them a dramatic and violent symphony, which his people could not resist."

Although the S.A., set up by Röhm, was affiliated to the Party, it did not come under Hitler's authority. All its cadres consisted of veteran

---

[1] *Baltikum* (Ed. Laffont)

volunteer corps officers, who had very little respect for the finesse of politics. Its commander-in-chief, Lieutenant-Colonel Hermann Kriebel, expressed this point of view with typically military plain-speaking: "The best thing political blokes can do would be to belt up."

At the beginning of 1923, one of Hitler's own appointees became head of the S.A., whereby he hoped to be able the better to control it. He was the war ace, Captain Hermann Goering, former commander of the famous Richthofen Squadron, decorated with the Order *Verdienstorden* (For Merit), the highest German military distinction. He had been exiled until 1922 and had thus had no contact with the volunteer corps. He was an epicurean, a lover of good food and good pictures, and he was a natural politician. He happened to hear Hitler by chance, one November evening in 1922, at the Königsplatz in Munich. He told his young wife the next morning: "I am all for that man."

Captain Hermann Goering, 26 years old, former Commander of the Richthofen Squadron, the most famous fighter squadron of the German Air Force, decorated with the Order, *Verdienstorden*. Leader of the S.A. in 1923.

Hitler put his trust in this man of politics, who vowed to him an unshakeable fidelity, in his conflict with the military clan of the S.A. From this opposition of temperament, ideas and method, was to be born in the future, after taking over power, the conflict with Röhm which would be decided in the bloody "Night of the Long Knives".

In spite of Goering's appointment, the S.A. in 1923 was far from being submissive. Its bellicose independence, upheld by the former leaders of the volunteer corps and by Röhm himself, impelled Hitler to set up a small troop of men, from outside the S.A., which would be entirely devoted to him.

This force, the *Stabswache* (Bodyguard), came to birth in March 1923. Its members swore an oath of loyalty to Hitler, and he, in turn, conferred upon them certain distinctive emblems. On the brown shirt of the S.A. they were to wear an armband underlined with two black bands; they also received a black helmet, on which shone a silver Death's Head.

The S.S. of the future was in embryo.

The Stosstruppe Adolf Hitler, the flag of the Ehrhardt Brigade and the armbands of the small Nazi party.

Julius Schreck, former officer of the Ehrhardt Brigade, the first leader of the Stosstruppe Adolf Hitler (which was the forerunner of the S.S.). He is seen here in his uniform as S.S. Standartenführer (Colonel) 1933.

Two months later, the *Stabswache* became the *Stosstruppe* (Assault Troop) *Adolf Hitler*. The name *Stosstruppe* harked back to the military formations which had led on to the volunteer corps; the admiration evoked by the *Stosstruppe* can be compared to that shown to commandos or parachutists. This formation was commanded by Lieutenant Berchtold and Captain Julius Schreck, a veteran of the Ehrhardt Brigade which had opted for Hitler against its former leader. Nevertheless, Schreck was faithful to his emblem. The *Stosstruppe Adolf Hitler* was to wear the armband with a swastika and carry the flag of the ex-Ehrhardt Brigade — as it happened, the flag of the former Imperial Navy.

The headquarters of the *Stosstruppe* was set up in the Torbräu public house. Round Julius Schreck were grouped the first members of Hitler's bodyguard; they were destined to remain faithful to him at all times and to follow his way up the political ladder. They consisted of Ulrich Graf, Emile Maurice, Christian Weber and Sepp Dietrich. All were united by a strong sense of camaraderie and by an absolute commitment – to protect the person whom they already called their *Führer*, even at the risk of losing their own lives.

This was no vague stylistic formula. Since the end of 1921, the Socialists and Communists had reorganised themselves, this having been made the easier by the fact that the conservative government, established by the volunteer corps in 1920, had had to resign. Their enemy number one was Hitler, who used their own methods against them and succeeded in reaching an understanding, not only with soldiers who had deserted but also with the ordinary people of Bavaria,

This illustration indicates the giddy devaluation of the Mark between 1920 and 1923: in 1920, a postcard cost 10 Pfennigs to send; in December 1923 the same postcard cost 10 million Marks. The Nazis were made to appear as the defenders of the middle classes who had been ruined by this catastrophe, in revolt against the wheeler-dealers who had built up a too-rapid fortune at their expense.

the workers and members of the middle classes. They were going to do all they could to break up the career of this dangerous competitor.

On 4th November 1921, the Communists and Socialists forced their way into a public meeting held by Hitler at the Hofbräuhaus. This was the baptism of fire for the young S.A. Although they shot only over the heads of the crowd, it was still a stunning reverse for the Marxists.

This set the tone. From now on, tension was only to mount. "You've got to make a nationalist belt up as soon as he opens his lying mouth," the Socialists proclaimed, and the Communists added: "Every public demonstration of the Nationalists must be immediately dispersed; the Nationalist assassins are outlaws from now on."

In point of fact, the Nazi Party was prohibited in a number of regions of Germany where the Socialists were dominant. In Bavaria, the S.A.'s answer to revolutionary violence was greeted as a salutary proof of their determination. One man finally came to the fore in the political arena to prove that the Reds would not be allowed to repeat unpunished the horrors of 1919.

On 9th November 1923, the Bavarian police shot at a procession led by Hitler and Ludendorff. This "Munich Putsch" was crushed in blood: sixteen dead members of the S.A. were stretched out on the road still gleaming from the melted snow; Hitler's bodyguards, Ulrich Graf and Josef Berchtold, were gravely wounded; the swastika standard bearer was in the death throes, staining the silk of the flag with his blood. This emblem was afterwards piously gathered up to become the *Blutfahne*, the Flag of Blood; it was passed over to the S.S. for safe keeping and was to emerge only when Hitler blessed the new S.S. and S.A. standards. The firing in the Feldherrnhalle at Munich finally put paid to the epic of the volunteer corps which had started, five years before to the day, with the revolution of 1918. The time for fighting-men was now passed, giving way to the politicians; but the latter were destined never to be able to free themselves from the imprint of those terrible years.

It was in world war, and later in civil war, that all the men who were going to play a part in the victory of the Nazi Party were shaped. When the curtain went up in 1919, the stage was already set; it was that of German misery and the street battles between the Reds and the volunteer corps, a struggle to the death between two conceptions of the world. The actors were in their places, but they did not yet know each other. The blind hand of Destiny was to push them towards each other.

Corporal Hitler was then 30, Captain Goering 26, Lieutenant Rudolf Hess 25, Lieutenant-Commander Canaris and Captain Röhm 32, the Volunteers Bormann and Himmler 19 and Reinhard Heydrich, a member of the Volunteer Corps of Halle, 16.

It was in this overheated atmosphere that the young Heinrich Himmler came of age. He had been a volunteer at the age of 17, but the War was to finish before his own education. He knew the front only from the last days of all, in 1918, but he was to join in the activity of the Bavarian Volunteer Corps. At the time of the Munich Putsch, he was carrying the *Reichskriegsflagge* (Reich Flag of War) and he took possession of the Bavarian War Ministry at the side of his leader, Captain Röhm.

The future cadres of the S.S. all passed through the same school. Obviously, the list is interminable, but we may mention among them Major Hubertus von Aulock, the famous volunteer corps leader, future *Brigadeführer* of the N.S.K.K.; Friedrich-Wilhelm Brückner, veteran of the von Epp Volunteer Corps, future *Obergruppenführer* (Lieutenant-General) S.S.; Kurt Daluege, veteran officer of the

The young S.A. apprentice, Heinrich Himmler, standard bearer of the *Reichskriegsflagge*, at the time of the Munich Putsch, 9th November 1923.

Rossbach Volunteer Corps, a future S.S. *Gruppenführer* (Major-General) and head of the Security Police; Sepp Dietrich, veteran of the *Oberland* Volunteer Corps, destined to become *Oberstgruppenführer* (Colonel-General) and one of the most famous generals of the Waffen S.S.; Karl Fritsch, a member of the von Epp Volunteer Corps and a future *Brigadeführer* (Brigadier) S.S.; Lieutenant F. W. Krüger, veteran of the Lützow Volunteer Corps, later to become *Höherer S.S. – und Polizeiführer* (Senior S.S. and Police Leader) for the Baltic countries. The same goes for Hermann Priess, who enlisted in the volunteer corps at the age of 17 and finished by becoming *Obergruppenführer* (Lieutenant-General) of the Waffen S.S.; Fritz von Scholz, of the von Epp Volunteer Corps, with the rank of *Gruppenführer* (Major-General) at the time of his death in 1944; Major Felix Steiner, ex-officer of the Märker Volunteer Corps, who later became the first instructor of the Waffen S.S. and attained the rank of *Obergruppenführer* (Lieutenant-General); Captain Karl Wolff, ex-officer of the Hesse Volunteer Corps, who became Himmler's adjutant;

The Oberland Volunteer Corps files past Hitler, marked with an X, at Munich in 1923.

Nazism was born of German misery after the defeat and the revolution of 1918. This is a poster exalting the popular resistance to the occupation of the Ruhr by the French troops in 1923. The caption reads: "*No! Make me if you can.*"

and Lieutenant Udo von Woysch, leader of the Silesian Volunteer Corps, who became S.S. *Obergruppenführer* (Lieutenant-General).

These were, in their own words, "hard men in hard times" – men of war, men of prey, picked out by a pitiless age in history. Pitiless they often were with each other; they were always pitiless with their enemies, right to the end of their bloody careers. To underline all these facts is not to seek an excuse for their actions; they themselves never sought any justification when they had to pay the price for their deeds. The historian may well pass value-judgements, but he must above all remember history as it was at the time it was lived. The history of the S.S. is unexplicable if we ignore the womb which brought it to birth and if we fail to penetrate the Germany which was being slowly martyred in the Twenties. This is what Georges Bernanos saw so clearly, when he wrote that the power of Hitler and his men "was born of German humiliation, of Germany trodden in the dust, decomposed, liquefied, in 1922. It bore the imprint of German misery, transfigured by despair, the face of German debauchery, at a time when the innumerable and untouchable reporters from both worlds paid for the hideous pleasure of seeing the sons of the dead heroes dance before them, painted, powdered, scented, swinging their hips – with an empty belly".[1]

---

[1] *Les grands cimetieres sous la lune* (*"The Vast Cemeteries in the Moonlight"*) (Ed. Plon, 1938).

The *Blutfahne* (Flag of Blood) of the Munich Putsch. It was put in the safekeeping of the S.S. on 4th July 1926.

CHAPTER 2

Your Honour is Your Loyalty

Birth of the S.S. (1924–1932)

The reverse experienced at the Munich Putsch and Hitler's imprisonment, followed by his trial and condemnation, far from harming the cause of the Party and its leader, merely served to get them better known and give them national importance. Where their influence had hitherto been restricted to Bavaria, it was now on the point of extending to the whole of the Reich. However, there were still plenty of troubles ahead.

The S.A. was dissolved. Röhm managed to get out of prison quickly, thanks to his contacts in the Army, and immediately undertook to set up a new front of former volunteer corps comrades and various political/military organisations. He was an incorrigible conspirator, who could never conceive of political action devoid of a subversive element. He set up the so-called *Frontbann*, incorporating the clandestine S.A. in it. Its success was immediate, because Röhm was a born organiser.

In prison, Hitler worked out quite a different strategy. He laid it all out in detail in *Mein Kampf*, which was to become the bible of his movement. Power was to be won by legal methods. He would come to power supported by a majority of Germans, with the help of political activity and propaganda.

When he came out of prison in 1924, Hitler was, thus, obviously in opposition to Röhm. He was quite willing to have an S.A., but only on

Members of the first S.S. in 1925, standing round Hitler. From left to right: Schaub, Schreck, Maurer, Schneider. The uniform is that of the S.A., consisting of brown breeches and shirt. However, the armband has two black stripes, and the helmet, black as well, is embossed with the Death's Head in silver.

condition that this organisation was a political formation, not a military force; above all, it had to be subject to the Party.

There was no immediate problem, since the S.A. was still dissolved. However, when Hitler re-constituted his Party in 1925 and once more went in for meetings and demonstrations, he needed the support of a pugnacious, disciplined and courageous organisation. His communist and socialist adversaries had not disarmed and they fully meant to prevent his speaking. The Party could not, then, do without a proper self-defence organisation.

Hitler commissioned the former head of the *Stosstruppe* (Storm Troop) to organise this new bodyguard. This was called the *Schutzstaffel* (Defence Squadron).* From it came the inspired

---

* The name of *Sturmstaffel* (Storm Squadron) was also used. Both these names rapidly ceased to be used in favour of the striking abbreviation: S.S.

abbreviation "S.S.", accompanied by an equally inspired double use of the old runic S, the flash of lightning symbolising victory. The name became official on 9th November 1925.

From the start, it was laid down that the S.S., unlike the S.A., should never become a mass organisation. It was accepted that the numbers would remain small, but its members would be men in whom total confidence could be placed.

With Hitler's approval, Julius Schreck ordered each local section of the N.S.D.A.P. on 21st September to set up an S.S. group of ten members, commanded by an experienced leader. Only Munich and Berlin were authorised to form several of these groups.

Captain Schreck was very careful about the men he chose. They had to be sturdy fellows, capable of standing up to much greater numbers of opponents. He never allowed them to step out of line. Not for him men who could only prop up bars, not for him pedestrian yes-men, not the unemployable! They had to be hard, sober, disciplined, devoted enough to die for their beliefs – these were the first men of the S.S. They had to be 23 at least and no more than 35. They had to be presented by two sponsors, who answered for them.

They were given the distinctive signs which were already in use for the first *Stabswache* (Bodyguard) of 1923: an armband with black stripes and a black helmet, distinguished by the Death's Head in silver, which had been taken from the *Baltikum* Volunteer Corps and the

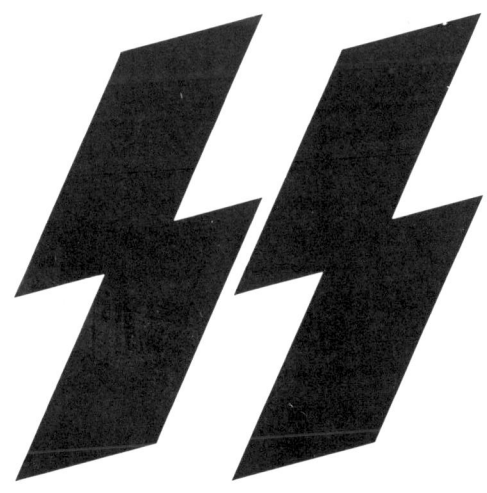

The emblem of the S.S., a double runic S, the solar symbol which expressed the idea of victory.

famous Black Hussars of the former Imperial Cavalry. They were fond of singing, as had the *Schwarze Totenkopfhusaren* (the Black Death's Head Hussars) been before them:

> *In black we are dressed*
> *In blood we are draped*
> *Death's Head on our helmet*
> *Hurrah! Hurrah!*
> *We stand unshaken.*

S.S. Member Alois Rosenwinck, Schreck's Adjutant, was talking seriously when he said: "The Death's Head should serve as a warning to our enemies, as a sign of the gift of our lives that we make to our Führer and his ideals."

More than one of them, indeed, was to lose his life in the struggle for power, convinced as they were that even if the right to be heard depended on majorities at the polling booths, cudgels and pistols still had very persuasive voices.

The first to fall was a student, Edgar Steinbach, mortally wounded by a pistol-shot aimed at him by the Communists at Chemnitz.* Hitler was quickly at his side. The dying man saluted him with outstretched arm and fell back dead.

It was at Dresden in 1925 that the new S.S. had its first opportunity to distinguish itself. Later, it was at Chemnitz, in Saxony. It was a bold stroke to hold a public meeting in this Red territory, but Hitler's audacious stake proved to be justified. In anticipation of trouble, Schreck had gathered together S.S. troops from Chemnitz, Dresden, Plauen and Zwickau, making up some 50 men. They had to face some several hundreds of counter-demonstrators, armed with iron bars and knives. They taught them such a lesson that Hitler's meetings in this region henceforth were conducted without opposition.

In April 1926, Josef Berchtold, wounded and sought by the police after the Munich Putsch, came to the surface again. He replaced Julius Schreck, who was nominated personal bodyguard/driver to Hitler. At this time, the S.S. numbered about 1000 men.

---

* Chemnitz is today called Karl-Marx Stadt.

ussar with Death's Head
(Totenkopfhusar), 1741.

Black Hussars with Death's Head (*Schwarze Totenkopfhusaren*), 1813.

Kolback of an officer of the Death's Head Hussars (*Totenkopfhusaren*) 1912 model, made of grey opposum and Death's Head made of silver (Gazette des Armes).

Kolback of reserve officer of 17th Regiment of Hussars, which was called the "Brunswick Hussars".

Detail of Death's Heads (*Totenköpf*) of the Imperial Hussars.

Officer of the Death's Head Hussars, aide-de-camp to the Kaiser William II.

43

The first S.S. troops adopt the Death's Head as their distinctive symbol.

On 4th July 1926 Hitler solemnly handed over the Flag of Blood, the *Blutfahne*, from the Munich Putsch to the safe-keeping of the S.S.

Nevertheless, despite the extension of its numbers, the S.S. remained a limited organisation, by reason of the rigorous selection procedures. It was not meant to offer a welcome to the large numbers of former volunteer corps members and the young nationalists, seduced by the para-military slogans. Most of the restrictions which had been made upon the S.A. had now been lifted, on the other hand, and it was therefore time to reconstruct it, turning it into a powerful mass organisation.

Hitler called upon one of the leading former heads of the *Baltikum* Volunteer Corps to lead the new S.A.; this was Captain Franz Pfeffer von Salomon, a relative of the French author of this book. He had also fought in Upper Silesia and in the Ruhr, where a French court martial had condemned him to death. Under his direction, the new S.A. rapidly

Captain Franz Pfeffer von Salomon, former head of the *Baltikum* Volunteer Corps, re-organised the S.A. in 1926 and was to lead it till 1930. He is here seen in conversation with Hitler, who is carrying his rhinoceros-skin hunting-crop.

grew, but, Prussian as he was, von Salomon took great exception to the autonomy of the S.S. He intended that the re-born S.A. should absorb the S.S.

Lieutenant Berchtold preferred resignation to accepting the conditions laid down by von Salomon. He was replaced by another veteran of the *Stosstruppe*, Erhard Heiden. The numbers of the S.S. fell to 280.

Though these numbers were small, the members of the S.S. were to cultivate their sense of élitism – summed up in the motto adopted: "Nobility is seen, not heard." They paid a heavier subscription than the other members of the Party, and had to buy their own uniforms. They were given the most humdrum jobs, to distribute tracts or to sell in public the Party organ, the *Völkischer Beobachter*, a job that they were expected to carry out with as much concentration and seriousness of purpose as a military operation. They thought of themselves as soldiers. Thus, they deliberately refrained from political discussion within the Party. They had but a single thought, centring round the Führer. In meetings, they were not allowed to smoke or move about. Their rigid attitude, their correct bearing and their constant sang-froid were meant "to serve as a political lesson for civilians". In everything, even in the most humble jobs, they were to set an example.

A strict code of rules fixed in detail all the behaviour of the S.S. while carrying out their missions, ranging from how to carry the S.S. identity card and the song book to the way of marching into a meeting. As Hitler was always very concerned to keep within the law, whatever the individual members of the S.S. might themselves have preferred, they never carried weapons; this was designed to prevent any cause for provocation – quite different from the S.A., who as always, carried their trusted Lügers and refused to be separated from them.

Such a rigid discipline even impressed the opposition. In 1929, a Bavarian police report noted with admiration: "At the smallest departure from the rules, a fine is imposed on the man, his armband is taken away from him or he is excluded from all activity for a time.

Hitler in 1926, surrounded by his S.S. bodyguard. On his right is Lieutenant Josef Berchtold (seated) and, in front, also seated, we see Heinrich Hoffmann, the Führer's official photographer.

Heinrich Himmler, the young *Reichsführer* of the S.S. (*Publisher Ullstein Verlag*).

Individual conduct and dress are at all times the object of constant attention." (Quoted by Heinz Hohne, "The Black Order", Casterman, 1968).

Adjutant Erhard Heiden was the patient and unbending architect of this education. When the S.S. grumbled about the hardships of their service and the lack of glamour, he was often heard to say: "The S.A. is just a band of men, but the S.S. is the Guard. There has always been a Guard. The Persians had one, and the Greeks, and Caesar and Napoleon, and old Fritz (Frederick the Great). The S.S. is the Guard of the new Germany."

On 6th January 1929, Hitler appointed a Commander to the S.S. with the title of *Reichsführer*; he was 29, and had the mild appearance of a short-sighted Japanese. He was called Heinrich Himmler.

This rather nondescript-looking man was the son of a respected teacher, former tutor to the Wittelsbach family, and his godfather was Prince Luitpold. He was a member of the best Bavarian society, coming from a cultivated family which was receptive to all intellectual movements, but was still traditionalist. He was a monarchist and a Catholic, as were most people in Bavaria. As his ambition was to become an officer, he joined up at the age of 17 as soon as war broke out. He was selected to become an officer cadet, and he was sent to the Front at the moment when the armistice was signed. He just had time to receive his baptism of fire.

There was little room in the defeated and revolutionary Germany of 1919 for a military calling, so Heinrich Himmler turned to the second resource of the nobility: the land. He became an agriculture student. As was usual, he joined a student fraternity; he drank only a little – to the great disgust of his comrades – but got his own back when it came to sabre-fights, receiving the regulation scars and, incidentally, thereby came into conflict with the Catholic Church, which condemned these pagan revivals.

An internal meeting of the young Nationalist Socialist Party, after its re-constitution in 1925. To the left of Hitler we see Gregor Strasser and Himmler.

Part of the Hitler legend concerns the pilgrimage made to the prison at Landsberg, where he was an inmate in 1924.

This was the start of the long journey which was to lead this young mystic to exchange the Judaic Christian God for the Germanic gods.

This inner conflict did not make him for a moment forget his penchant for the military. He joined a volunteer corps, one of those set up in Bavaria to crush the Reds; then, later, he was active in a companion troop to the S.A., the *Reichskriegsflagge* (War Flag of the Reich – not to be confused with the *Reichsflagge*, the Reich Flag, which was reactionary and hostile to the Nazis), led by the ebullient Captain Röhm; he also joined the N.S.D.A.P. He took part in the Munich Putsch as standard-bearer of the *Reichskriegsflagge*.

The failure of the Munich Putsch did not put him off. While Ernst Röhm was imprisoned, he met a pharmacist at Landshut, Gregor Strasser, who represented the left wing of the movement and was gathering around him the remnants of the National Socialist Party. Himmler took it upon himself to reorganise the Party in Lower Bavaria and to prepare for the elections of 1924. He spent his time patrolling the countryside on an old motor bike to indoctrinate the peasants. He was a model recruit. Gregor Strasser once told his brother Otto: "I've

The Nazis believed the Jews – the masters, according to them, of the Weimar Republic – were behind the police repression which hit them so hard during the time when they were fighting for power. The person represented on this caricature is the socialist Prefect of Police at Berlin, Bernhard Weiss, later nicknamed by Goebbels "Isidor" (*a drawing by Mjolnir in* Der Angriff, *a newspaper published in Berlin by Goebbels*).

never seen a lad with such a thirst for action. He's got to be responsible for something all the time – it doesn't matter what. To be able to spread his wings, he's got to be doing something which goes far beyond any personal little project. He's got a constant thirst for consecration."

The members of his family had long been saying – and the students' fraternity repeated it frequently: "Heinrich will see to it!"

There were other people too who appreciated that Heinrich would tackle anything, and do so with great exactitude, ever searching for perfection in detail.

He was one of the first to join the S.S. He was very well aware that nothing great or durable can be created without the presence of an élite; how could he fail to consider himself destined to fulfil this role? In 1925, he was *Gauleiter* (Regional Governor) of Lower Bavaria. The following year, he became responsible for propaganda throughout the Reich, at first under Strasser's orders, and then, directly under Hitler's (from 1928 onwards).

Once he had become the Führer's direct partner, he persisted in putting before his leader his idea of an élite force within the Party, later destined to become an élite for the whole of Germany, and one which would be as devoted to the Führer as formerly the Jesuits had been to the Pope. This concept was not displeasing to Hitler, who was to say later: "It's thanks to Himmler that the S.S. has become this extraordinary organisation, devoted to one idea and faithful to death. Himmler strikes me as our Ignatius Loyola. He's used all his intelligence and pertinacity, and has faced wind and high water, to forge this instrument."

Heinrich had found a new mission: the *Reichsführer's* S.S. would set up a new religion. His new beliefs complemented very well the more ancient ones held by Hitler. He was to be the founder of a new Church, an Order, of which the Führer was to be the inspired prophet. Both were united in a *Weltanschauung* (concept of the world) which dominated their political mission from on high.

... "In the beginning was ice. And the wind blew through the leafless branches of the immense forests. But then came a fire in the

Richard Wagner.

night of the great North. Men stole this image of the sun and adored it as the embodiment of their God. This is how, for Heinrich Himmler, *Reichsführer* S.S., the history of the world began. Light and life did not come from the East, but from the North, the country of glaciers and torrents, where night never seems to finish throughout the winter. Amid this wild and grandiose nature was born a race of men with blond hair and light eyes." (Quotation from Henri Landemer, *La Waffen S.S.*)

They sculpted in stone the flaming solar cross and lit huge beacons from hill to hill, during the summer solstice, to broadcast the joyous message of life. From the dawn of history, they leapt forward to conquer the world, riding in their light chariots, drawn by frisky horses, and sailing in their fine deep sea ships. They bore aloft the sword of bronze and the rapier of steel. In successive waves they swept over Europe and pushed far into the East. The shock of their youth and the power of their superior arms crushed the old dormant empires. On the smoking ruins, they founded their kingdoms, built their towns and sowed their fields.

But then, in the course of the centuries, the most noble and most ancient of those peoples, the Hellenes, the Celts and the Romans, appeared to have been struck by an insidious disease: their men laid low the sword and their women turned their faces away from the cradles. Enervated by the perfidious music of sages and merchants from the East, poisoned by a gospel of despair and death, the children of the Sun turned their backs on their gods. The gods had taken refuge in the German forest. But then they lit new fires within the heart of a strong people. The solar cross once more resumed its conquering course over the world. As long as there are men of good race, life cannot die.

Onto the "Aryan myth" of Gobineau and Chamberlain, the *Reichsführer* S.S. grafted the pan-Germanist theories of the last century, brought up to date by *Mein Kampf* and the three party doctrinaires, the philosopher Alfred Rosenberg, the ethnologist Hans Günther and the agronomist Walter Darré. Henri Landemer noted that Himmler owed to those sources what was to constitute the trilogy of the S.S.: A non-Christian religious sense, the consciousness of Nordic race and the ideas of nobility and "roots".

Against Christian virtues, Himmler opposed his Teutonic values – dignity instead of a sense of sin and racial solidarity instead of love of one's neighbour. To the Catholic liturgy he was to oppose that of the S.S. Order.

Houston Stewart
Chamberlain (*Ullstein*).

Josef Arthur de Gobineau
(*Süd-Verlag*).

In 1930 he restored the ancient celebration of the winter solstice and instituted the feast of Yuletide in place of the Christian Christmas. In 1931 he issued the Ordinances concerning the marriage of men belonging to the S.S.

But this mystic dreaming did not distract him from more immediate tasks. Germany was in the grip of an economic crisis and a new period of distress threatened. Violence was reborn in the streets and the fear of a Red revolution once more hovered over the Reich. A new chance was being offered to the young infantrymen in the brown shirts and the black tunics. Neither Hitler nor his faithful Heinrich had any intention of letting the opportunity pass.

In April 1929, Himmler persuaded Hitler and Franz Pfeffer von Salomon to accept a recruiting plan, designed to create a true Order out of the S.S. Only properly selected candidates would be accepted, and the first criterion was to be race.

Let us listen to what Himmler himself said in a speech he made to the officers of the Wehrmacht in January 1937. He said: "I am convinced of the reality of this concept of the world, namely, that, in the end, only pure blood can bring about a firm and durable government. History teaches us indeed that only those born of pure race are capable of directing and creating – particularly those who have Nordic blood. I decided some time ago, that, if ever I succeeded in uniting in a single organisation a large number of German men possessing that blood, in making them submit to military obedience and in teaching them the

The Fourth *Parteitag* (Party Conference) in August 1929. The *Blutfahne* and its S.S. Guard. Himmler can be seen in the background. Apart from the black helmet and the armband with its black stripes, the uniform then comprised breeches and boots in the same colour. The collar insignia, indicating the rank, were also just making their appearance.

Rigorous selection.

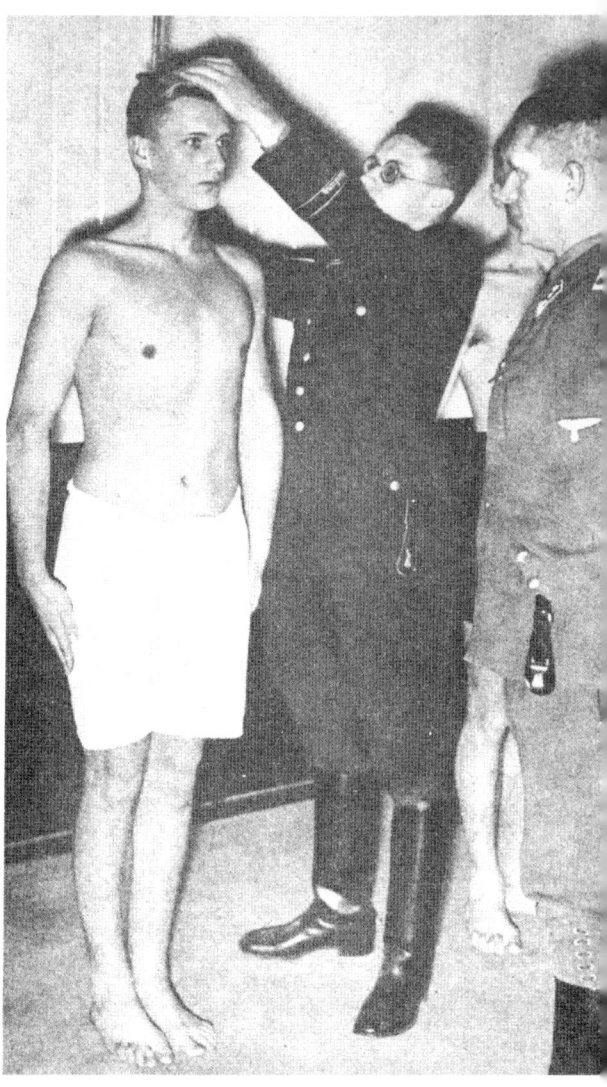

importance of their Nordic origins and of the *Weltanschauung* they would have as a consequence, then it would be possible to create and organise an élite capable of standing up to any trial.

This selection on the basis of pure race has already been very often recognised in theory. There are quite a number of books on this question, ranging from Chamberlain's to Günther's. The most difficult question was that of selection. There are two ways in which you can select: the harder one is the one that results from a war or from a decisive struggle. By this method, pure race proves itself by good results. In 1929 we still had numbers of veterans whose attitude during the War had proved their true value. But wars are passing events, and it was necessary to find a way of handling the problem of selection during peace also, a time when the personal experience of courage cannot exist.

It would seem that I was forced to base my judgement upon external appearances i.e. what sort of man each one seemed to be, but then I should have immediately laid myself open to criticism: 'All that is very well and good', people would have said, 'but it's a very dubious technique to go on size, the colour of fair hair and blue eyes, even the skull'. I was very well aware of all that. I decided this method alone could not solve my problem. I did at first demand a certain height: I would not take any men who were less than 1 metre 70 (= 5′ 5″) tall, because I knew that tallness is a sign of good blood. Then I demanded photographs, and by this means I was able to accept from 100 to 200

Certificate awarded by the Third Reich to former members of a volunteer corps. The wording on the Certificate is as follows:

Certificate. The Reich and Prussian Minister of the Interior has instructed me to issue the present Certificate which confirms that .... participated in the struggles of the .... Volunteer Corps. The Reich hereby expresses its gratitude and recognition that he voluntarily defended and protected the German Reich at a critical period by risking his life and limbs. Berlin, 23rd April 1936. Signed by the Bundesführer of the German Imperial War Veterans' Association.

men a year. I myself looked at all the photographs of candidates, and I always asked myself the question: does this man have any signs of inferior blood, for example, do his cheek bones protrude – which would indicate that he was of mongol or slavonic origin? I never forgot my experience of the members of the Soldiers' Councils from 1918 to 1919. Any one of you, who was an officer at that time, will remember that these men looked very peculiar, from a German point of view: they had strange features and often gave the impression of being foreigners; it was the type of man whom you could very well recruit and lead in peace time – he'd even show himself quite courageous and daring in war – but, when the worst comes to the worst, when his character and nerves are strained to the utmost, his blood will betray him.

Knowing all this as I did, I undertook to accept no-one who was not absolutely safe from the point of view of blood or anyone who, in the moment of an attack, would be revealed to be a discontented or disloyal person or who was capable of going over to the enemy, of grumbling or, in general, of reminding us too well of the behaviour of the Soldiers' Councils. This was all the more necessary in as much as, during the years of struggle, we had nothing but a voluntary discipline within the S.S. – we had no means of forcing our members. It was necessary that every man should voluntarily accept any punishment given to him, that he should of his own accord hand over his armband and should voluntarily do fatigues by way of punishment. But, if he was not prepared for this, he was able to leave freely. We, thus, followed this principle of selection, and we never made any very significant mistake. Nevertheless, I could not hope to find the true élite by relying on physical appearances only.

I kept to the principle that, if I wanted to attract men of worth, it was no good offering them an easy service and lots of fun, but, on the contrary, difficulties and stern trials. So, we demanded that our men buy their own black trousers and their boots, although this was an enormous expense for an out-of-work man, costing 40 Marks. If he told us that he couldn't be sure of being able to pay, then we replied: 'Sorry, mate, you don't understand. You've got to be ready for every sacrifice. Sorry we can't use you.' "

These standards had a great appeal to the veterans and young nationalists whom Himmler addressed. They were enthusiastic about the fundamental concept of the S.S. Order, which seemed to offer them straightaway a moral *revanche* over the trading and middle class society

Himmler at the *Parteitag* (Party Conference) of 1931, held at Bad Harzburg. On his right can be seen Ernst Röhm, the new commander of the S.A.

which had rejected them. Within the S.S., the customary concept of a social élite was replaced by that of a racial élite.

Veterans of the old volunteer corps were demanding men: the S.S. offered them a new Fatherland. They joined up in large numbers.

At the beginning of 1930, the S.S. had 2000 men. Pfeffer von Salomon was worried about this, but Hitler cut short the discussion by officially separating the S.S. from the S.A. while retaining the subordination of the former, at the administrative level, to the O.S.A.F.*, von Salomon. However, Hitler made quite clear his preferences in the words: "No S.A. officer is authorised to give orders to the S.S."

It was at this time, too, that the entirely black uniform was adopted to distinguish the S.S. Himmler gave as much attention to external symbols as does a stage director in a theatre. He reasoned that, even if

* Oberster S.A. Führer (Supreme S.A. Leader).

such objects cannot change the soul of a man, at least they give him an identity. They certainly promoted a fascination which was good for the recruitment of a certain élite.

The *Reichsführer* S.S. obtained Hitler's permission to cease to limit local groups to ten men. Better still, the S.A. was ordered to supply half the manpower of the new S.S. sections on the basis of the most careful hand-picking.

Thus, the S.S. structure was built on that of the S.A. The basic unit was the *Schar* (Squad), consisting of eight men commanded by a *Scharführer*. Three *Scharen* formed a *Trupp* (Troop), under the orders of a *Truppführer*. Three *Truppen*, made up of some 70 to 120 men, formed a *Sturm*, commanded by a *Sturmführer*. The *Stürme* were grouped in threes into a *Sturmbann*, the numbers of which varied between 250 and 600 men, under the orders of a *Sturmbannführer*. Above this, a number of *Sturmbanne* constituted a *Standarte* (Regiment), the commander of which was known as *Standartenführer* and which had some 1000 to 4000 men. Several *Standarten* were later grouped together, as recruitment proceeded, into an *Untergruppe* or *Brigade*, with a *Brigadeführer* at its head. Above this, a number of *Brigaden* sometimes formed a *Gruppe* (Division), under the command of a *Gruppenführer*. Subsequently, a new echelon was set up, the *Obergruppe* (Army Corps), with an *Obergruppenführer* at its head. Later still, the Waffen S.S. was to create the rank of *Oberstgruppenführer* (Colonel-General).

This was the highest rank of the S.S. hierarchy, apart from the one of *Reichsführer*, the Grand Master of the Order, reserved for Himmler. Sometimes, admittedly, these ranks were awarded to do honour to certain individuals, but they also could represent the importance attached to some function, not connected with the command of any particular military unit. We should be in no doubt that this military structure was above all aimed at catching the popular imagination and intended to impose a strict discipline. Himmler also established the intermediate rank of *Oberführer*, coming between those of *Standartenführer* (Colonel) and *Brigadeführer* (Brigadier).

Apart from the vertical hierarchy, there was also a horizontal hierarchy, corresponding to the territorial regions covered by the *Reichswehr* – *Gau*, (Region), *Kreiss* (County), *Abschnitt* (District).

The last of these corresponded to a military district. Here again the same deliberate militarism was recognisable, the more explicable

Walther Stennes, ex-officer of a volunteer corps, *Oberführer* of the S.A. at Berlin, headed the revolt of the "brown barons".

because many of the recruits were from former Army units. These men were unable to detach themselves from warfare, which had marked them permanently.

Whereas the S.S. grew, the S.A. proliferated. In the latter organisation, the criteria of selection were looser, because the purpose was to set up a mass organisation. As it necessarily embraced large numbers of out-of-work men who were recruited – 60% of the S.A. at Berlin came into this category – behaviour and discipline reflected this structure, even at the level of the leaders: the higher-ranking officers of the S.A. tended to think of themselves as feudal seigneurs of their domains. Their allegiance to the Party and the person of Hitler was strictly conditional.

In the North, indeed, the S.A. was subject to quite a serious split. It took very badly the arrival of a new Party head – the enterprising Dr. Goebbels. Faithful to a deep-seated German tradition, they scoffed at Bavarians. But there was a more sinister movement at work: under the influence of the Strasser brothers, the S.A. at Berlin deliberately went in for socialist demagogy – they used to say: "We're the proletariat, and Adolf is betraying us."

Others hawked around tracts containing words such as: "We, the proletariat, are practically starving, but our beloved Führer can afford to buy a Mercedes for 40,000 Marks."

Hitler went to Berlin to re-establish order. He came to an understanding with Walther Stennes, *Oberführer* of the S.A., a former volunteer corps officer and the author of the Putsch of the Black *Reichswehr* (an unsuccessful insurrection which had taken place in 1923). News was broadcast of their reconciliation on 1st September 1930.

Nevertheless, the S.A. was in full crisis. The military ideas of the O.S.A.F. and von Salomon clashed starkly with those of Hitler, who meant the S.A. to be subordinate to the Party. Pfeffer resigned, preferring this way out to rebellion. Hitler took matters into his own hands and demanded an oath of loyalty to his person from the leaders of the S.A. Then he sent a telegram to Röhm, who had become an instructor to the Bolivian Army. He recalled that the latter had said to him, just before leaving: "Just let me know the day, the hour and the place – I'll be there."

Despite a brilliant career in Bolivia, Röhm was homesick. His deepest sentiments were concerned with the humiliation of Germany, which he had vowed to avenge. At Hitler's call, he threw his things

Ernst Röhm, seen between Goering and Hitler.

together and took the first boat home. The S.A. was going to get a leader, capable of dealing with its astounding growth.

As soon as they felt the effects of his mailed fist, the S.A. leaders at Berlin rebelled. An internal putsch was in the air. It was the man in charge of the S.S. at Berlin, Kurt Daluege, who alerted Röhm and Hitler on 1st April 1931 in a secret report: "All the S.A. officers at Berlin have taken sides for Stennes against Hitler."

The next day, 2nd April, Stennes' men were in a state of rebellion. They chased Gauleiter Goebbels out of his office and took over the premises of his newspaper, *Der Angriff*. The putsch spread throughout the whole of Northern Germany. The S.A. leaders in Brandenberg, Hesse, Silesia, Pomerania and Mecklenburg, supported Stennes. Never before had the Party known such a crisis. Its foes, the Communists, Liberals and Socialists, rubbed their hands. Hitler's fall was widely prophesied.

Hitler, however, bided his time. The movement died as quickly as it had been born, lacking money. Goering received the order to purge the S.A. of Stennes' supporters, and ex-Lieutenant Paul Schultz, the redoubtable leader of the Upper Silesian Volunteer Corps, the former executioner of the *Vehme*, was given the job of re-organising the S.A. throughout the North. Hitler issued his public congratulations to the S.S., which alone had been opposed to this break-up. He wrote to Daluege: "Your honour is your loyalty."

Kurt Daluege in 1937.

The Leibstandarte S.S. presents arms to honour Hitler's arrival at Nuremberg for the 1934 Congress.

This slogan was taken up later to become the motto of the S.S.: *Meine Ehre heisst Treue* (My Honour is my Loyalty.)

During all this time, Himmler doubled his vigilance and the harshness of his rule within the S.S. The more the numbers grew, the stricter became the discipline. It was sufficient for a man to be three times absent without leave to be excluded forever. The exercises became ever more difficult.

The law of secrecy was tightened up. No one had the right to look into the affairs of the S.S. and every S.S. man was compelled to keep his mouth shut about everything that had to do with his duties. The men of the S.S. were also forbidden to participate in arguments with other members of the Party, even when they were attacked – in such circumstances, their instructions were to leave the meeting with the words: "We're only carrying out the Führer's orders."

CHAPTER 3

The New Inquisition

Taking Power and the Security Service (1932–1937)

From 1930 onwards, Himmler started collecting as much information as he could on the Party's enemies. People hostile to the N.S.D.A.P. were categorised as Communists, Freemasons or Jews. In every S.S. Section, Himmler set up an *Untergruppe*, specially charged with the job of learning about and spying on the enemies outside and within the Party.

In 1931, the S.S. was strengthened by an interesting personality, Reinhard Heydrich, who had recently joined the Party. Reinhard Tristan Heydrich was then 27. He was born in 1904 at Halle. His father was director of the conservatoire of music and a composer of operas. He himself studied music. He had exceptional intellectual ability, but was also an excellent sportsman, going in for fencing, sailing and swimming, in all of which he was something of an expert. At the age of 16, in 1920, he joined the volunteer corps which liberated his town, where the Reds had committed a number of atrocities. In 1922 he joined the Navy as a cadet. He served for some time under the orders of the future Admiral Canaris, who fully appreciated his abilities and his charm. His good looks and his success with women got him into a few scrapes. In April 1931 he was dismissed from the Navy for "bringing discredit upon it", after refusing to recognise his responsibility to the daughter of a shipbuilder, who declared that he had made her pregnant. So he was back in civilian life. He got engaged to Lina von Osten, and it was she who was to convert him to Nazism. She enlisted the help of a member of the S.S., Friedrich Karl von Eberstein, to bring him to Himmler's notice on 14th June 1931. Himmler received a favourable impression of Heydrich by reason of his Nordic physique and his intellectual strength. The interview was short. Himmler did not need long to sum up the potential of this new recruit. He went straight to the point: "I want to set up a security and information service within the S.S., and I need a specialist. If you think you could do this management job, will you please write down on paper how you think you would tackle it. I'll give you 20 minutes."

Heydrich knew very little about the matter, but his logical mind made it possible for him to sketch out a concise summary of what he would do. Himmler was extremely impressed. When the interview was

Reinhard Heydrich, an accomplished sportsman, of Nordic physique, keen intelligence and a will of iron – the very archetype of an S.S. man. Unable to attack him directly, his enemies tried to discredit him with the fable that his origin was Jewish.

over, he handed over to Heydrich the job of setting up the information and security service of the S.S., the *Sicherheitsdienst* or S.D.

His faith was fully justified: Reinhard Heydrich proved to be the man he needed for this job.

On 5th October 1931, Heydrich became a member of the S.S. After a short stay at the Brown House, he decided to set the S.D. up out of the sight of prying eyes. His analytical mind was matched by a remarkable perspicacity. He was able to knot and unknot the networks of relationships, and he made of the S.D. a model service. His rapid promotion proved how efficient he was, for honours rained upon him: on 10th August 1931 he became *Sturmführer*, on 1st December *Hauptsturmführer*, in July 1932 *Standartenführer* and in March 1933

Demonstration by the S.S. and the S.A. of Berlin in 1932, following on the street fights with the Reds, during which a number of their comrades were killed.

Oberführer. Originally, Heydrich's activity was limited to Bavaria, where it did much to increase the reputation of the S.S. Hitler himself acknowledged the value of this work.

On 25th January 1932, Hitler appointed Himmler as security chief for the Brown House, that is to say, the Head of the Party Police.

In October 1932, a scandal broke out in the S.A. Röhm's liking for young men was a topic of every conversation. He himself was not troubled by it — his virility did not suffer by it. He compared this tendency to the behaviour of some of the Spartan warriors. But such explanations had no effect on public opinion, the more so as a rather sordid financial affair was linked with these rumours.

The closer scandal got to the Brown masses, the more the puritanical rigour of the Black Order was encouraged and reinforced. Both within and without the Party, it was thought that only Himmler and the S.S. could clean the Augean stables within the S.A.

The first S.S. men to carry arms, in 1933 at Munich, in front of the Feldherrnhalle. Himmler had just been appointed Prefect of Police for the town.

But 1932 was not to be the year of purges. The Party first had to win power. After the economic crisis, the misery and the unemployment, the political struggle rapidly took on the character of an underground civil war. The Communist Party and the Socialists set up armed militias. However, the S.A. and the S.S. did not lag behind, and a number of them were to pay with their lives in this deadly struggle. Ten members of the S.S. were killed in 1932 and several hundreds wounded during scuffles with the Red militias. The violence and hatred that this created was to have a profound effect a few months later.

On the horns of an intolerable dilemma, the old Marshal von Hindenburg, President of the Reich, entrusted Hitler on 30th January 1933 with the responsibility of forming a government. The World War corporal was now realising the first of his dreams. He became Chancellor of the Reich, but this was only the first stage towards total revolution — a revolution which was to end in order.

Not everybody saw it in this light. The S.A. who marched in procession during the evening of 30th January throughout all the towns of Germany, accompanying the sound of their boots with their war cries, amounted to 400 000. A year later, they were to be 4 millions — 4 million men under the command of the former captain, Ernst Röhm. He, also, saw his dreams coming true — he was getting his revenge on the *Reichswehr* and he was settling the old volunteer corps accounts. What he really wanted to do was to construct a new Reich, of which the S.A. would be the overlords — a military Reich, a sort of vast camp, full of martial sounds and joyous songs. It was the dream of an adolescent, the dream of the poor bloody infantrymen. But neither the Party, nor the Reichswehr, nor even Hitler in the final analysis, shared Captain Röhm's hopes. All at once, Röhm felt himself both powerful and threatened. He sulked and grumbled; when he'd been drinking, he gave way to seditious statements, such as: "The Revolution won't be stopped in mid-course; the brown tide (the S.A.) will swamp the grey rock (the *Reichswehr*)."

On 28th February 1933, less than a month after the takeover of power the Reichstag was on fire. Was this an attempt at a Communist coup, or merely provocation? The very next day a decree was issued: "For the protection of the people and the State", giving police powers to the S.A. and the S.S., particularly of arresting suspects. Arms were issued to 25,000 S.A. and 15,000 S.S. Hitler gave orders to the S.S. to set up a special guard for his personal safety. His private detective, Sepp

The *Leibstandarte S.S. Adolf Hitler*, the first S.S. unit to officially bear arms and live in barracks, mounts guard in front of the Chancellery.

Dietrich, got together 120 hand-picked members of the S.S. This new so-called *Stabswache* (Bodyguard) went on guard at the Chancellery door. Its numbers grew. In the Congress of September 1933, the Führer presented the new unit with its flag, and gave it a new name: *Leibstandarte S.S. Adolf Hitler* (Personal Standard S.S. Adolf Hitler). The men in black were from now on never absent from Hitler's side.

At the same time, Goering, the Prime Minister of Prussia, was purging the police – a body in which the Socialists were numerous – and was setting up a department of information and political repression, the State Secret Police, *Geheime Staatspolizei*, abbreviated to Gestapo.

This initiative was scarcely calculated to please Himmler. As Grand Inquisitor, all the police forces should have been subject to him. To reach this position, he had found an ally in the person of the Minister of

Himmler, the new Head of the *Geheime Staatspolizei*, the Gestapo, talking to his predecessor, Rudolph Diehls, faithful friend of Goering and hostile to the S.S.

the Interior, Dr. Wilhelm Frick. Frick was a confirmed enemy of the autonomy of the *Länder* (Provinces). He was a politician who believed in centralisation. The whole of the Reich should have but one law, and Himmler added: "And one police". Dr. Frick nodded his head.

Discreetly, thanks to Dr. Frick's help, the police forces of the *Länder* fell one by one under Himmler's authority. In January 1934, when Frick laid before Hitler his Bill for the administrative reorganisation of the Reich, Himmler was in charge of all the police forces of Germany, except for the most powerful of all, the one in Prussia.

This time Goering had to yield, but he did not do so without expressing his doubts. The enormous development of the S.A. and the bellicose spirit which animated both it and its leader seemed to him to constitute a danger of such exceptional gravity for the stability of a National Socialist regime, which was still fragile, that he felt the S.S. was the only existing force capable of opposing the S.A. So he made the sacrifice of his police.

Himmler asserted that he always gave the most offensive security jobs to the best men. Here we see three non-commissioned officers of the S.S. *Sonderkommando Sachsen* (S.S. Special Commando Unit, Saxony) at the gateway to a concentration camp.

Now the S.S. controlled all the German police forces. Himmler, who had been the poor relation when jobs were handed out immediately following the taking of power – all he got was the Prefecture of Police at Munich – could now congratulate himself on his patience and his prudent conduct.

On 10th April 1934 he entered Number 8, Prinz-Albert-Strasse, the headquarters of the Gestapo, as its chief – it now came under the authority of the S.D. and its leader, Reinhard Heydrich.

After the *Leibstandarte S.S. Adolf Hitler*, the first S.S. formation to be armed and to live in barracks, Himmler set up other armed bodies, such as the *S.S. Sonderkommando* and the *Politische Bereitschaften* (Political Reserves). These formations went into action for the first time in 1933, at a time when there were bloody encounters, fomented by the Communists.

To answer the threat of violent subversion, he set up near Dachau an internment camp, the first of the *Konzentrationslager* – K.Z. (Concentration Camps), which were to acquire such a sinister reputation during the Second World War. At this time, however, the camp regime, and that of those which were about to open shortly after in other parts to confine and "educate" the enemies of the new Reich, was still comparatively agreeable. Special units, the *Totenkopfverbände* (the Death's Head Companies), were given the job of guarding the camps; however, they were soldiers rather than warders. Himmler always reckoned on entrusting the most unpleasant jobs, connected with the security of the Reich, to the best men he had. Later, that was to change.

The men of the *S.S. Totenkopfverbände* were very young. They were given an intense sporting, military and political training, and they carried arms. Their official mission was to mount guard outside the camps. The whole administration and internal policing of the camps rested on the horrible system of *Kapos*, that is to say, leaders chosen from the inmates themselves. It was the Communists who rapidly achieved power inside the camps, exercising pitiless controls over the other inmates.

The Head of the *S.S. Totenkopfverbände* was the Brigadeführer Theodor Eicke, an ex-officer from the First World War. He had gone into the *Schutzpolizei* (Protection Police), which did not exactly have a reputation for tenderness. He soon built up three *Standarte* (Regiments), to which he gave the names of German provinces:

Himmler was as yet still only the brilliant second-in-command to Röhm. He arranged his "cards" carefully, held them close to his chest and waited.

S.S. Brigadeführer, Theodor Eicke, the creator of the *S.S. Totenkopfverbände*, S.S. units carrying the Death's Head as their badge, whose job it was to guard the concentration camps.

Oberbayern (Upper Bavaria) at Dachau, *Brandenburg* at Oranienburg and *Thüringen* (Thuringia) at Buchenwald.

Whereas the S.S. held its fire and bided its time, paying attention to the quality of its recruitment by a constant purging process, the S.A. threw its weight about noisily. Around the person of Röhm, all the talk was about the "Second Revolution", which was to sweep away the bourgeois in the Party and the reactionaries from the *Reichswehr*. Their street processions, jazzed up by a few drunkards, were accompanied by their favourite song:

> *"We're going to sharpen our long knives*
> *Along the pavement's edge."*

Unfortunately for them, these empty words were seized on with great seriousness by the *Reichswehr*, which called upon Hitler to intervene. The Führer could not refuse the request. Ever since November 1918, the *Reichswehr* had been the very incarnation of the continuity of the Reich, which had been maintained despite revolution, the civil war and the vicissitudes of defeat. When the time came for old Marshal Hindenburg to disappear, Hitler knew he would not get supreme power without the backing of the *Reichswehr*. The latter used its position to bargain. The Führer had to take a decision – the Army or the S.A.

The pretext was given by Goering, Goebbels and Himmler. Quite apart from the misunderstandings and conflicts which made them antagonistic to Röhm, the security and the whole future of the Third Reich were at stake. Himmler was the most difficult of the three to be brought round to accept a violent solution – he retained a sincere liking for his former leader. But the danger was too great – not, perhaps, of a putsch, but, still more serious, of disorder created by the very men who should have been setting the example of good order. Their incessant stepping out of line, the brawls, the drinking sessions, the gratuitous violence, the arbitrary arrests, the incendiary statements and irresponsible conversations of leaders of the S.A. provoked profound discontent in public opinion. The confidence the Germans had in the new regime was in danger of collapsing.

The situation seemed irredeemable – neither advice nor discussion was capable of convincing Röhm and his men. When they sulked, 4 million super-rowdies, more or less armed and unassailable, sulked with them. The Third Reich was inextricably sliding down towards anarchy.

30th June 1934 was the decisive day. Goering, Goebbels and Himmler convinced Hitler of the imminence of an S.A. plot. This invention by the S.D. was the only way they had of forcing the Führer to make up his mind. But, once he had taken the decision, there was no stopping him. Trembling with feverish anger, he personally directed the operations at Munich and Bad Wiessee, where the heads of the S.A. had peacefully gathered together at his request.

It was the men of the *S.S. Leibstandarte*, the *Totenkopfverbände* and the *Sonderkommando* who were called upon to carry out the arrests and the executions.

Hitler could not do without the *Reichswehr*, because that organisation was the personification of the legitimacy of the State. He decided to break the bullying spirit of the S.A. by the bloody "Night of the Long Knives" in order to retain the friendship of the *Reichswehr*.

The *S.S. Sonderkommandos*, an auxiliary military police, under Himmler's orders. Its members took part in the "Night of the Long Knives".

The S.A. was decapitated. Most of those who fell under the bullets of the S.S. were former volunteer corps leaders – adventurers, it is true, but also indefatigable warriors, better at taking government by storm than organising it.

The S.S. seized the opportunity to settle its scores with its enemies. The former Bavarian Prime Minister, von Kahr, who had smashed the Munich Putsch 11 years earlier, was found in a peat pit with his skull staved in. He was more than 80 years old. General von Schleicher, who had tried to obstruct the Party's rise to power in 1932, was murdered, along with his wife. Von Papen's private secretary was executed as a warning to his master. Finally, Otto Strasser, the left-wing Nazi, an old companion in the struggle but one who had opposed it from inside, was also sacrificed.

A hundred or so victims were to pay with their lives in this bloody purge. The exact number of executions was never known, but Heinz Höhne estimated it at 84.

The "Night of the Long Knives" had one unforeseen consequence: it consecrated the new power of the S.S. The action of that night gave the S.S. an awesome reputation, which it used to impose its strength still further. With discretion and patience, it built up a pitiless military and religious Order, the command posts of which were guarded by the survivors of the volunteer corps. Out of the revolutionary dream, born in the *Baltikum*, the S.S. was to construct reality.

Let us now study the words of the founder of the S.S., *Reichsführer S.S.* Heinrich Himmler. In a long speech before the officers of the Wehrmacht, in January 1937, Himmler gave a detailed study of the organisation and missions of the S.S., some time before the Black Order was to become, with the incidence of war, a monstrous empire. It should be noted that the whole of the rest of the present chapter is taken up with extracts from that speech.

1. *The Formation and Training of the S.S.*

"In 1933, the S.S. was going through a crucial period. It was the time of rapid development of all the Party organisations. We were faced by a most difficult problem: we had to choose between closing the doors of the Party and its constituent elements, retaining a unit of the highest quality but with very few followers and a restricted base, or else opening up the structural units in order to enlarge our base. This second solution, the one we adopted, brought into the Party a large number of people who were neither really enthusiastic or idealistic; – such people, by reason of their very numbers, endangered us all. For this reason, while the other structural units of the Party were being enlarged, I shut the doors on the S.S. in 1933. Between the years 1933 and 1935, I swept out all those who had no value for us, excluding some 60,000 members, whereas the actual numbers of the S.S. in 1937 were only 210,000. This purge was of immense value to the Order. Quality improved to the detriment of quantity.

Today, when a young man of 20 comes forward, we know him because he's been through the Hitler Youth. We examine him and we observe him for a number of years. Only 15 out of 100 candidates are accepted. We demand a political certificate in respect of his parents, his brothers and his sisters. We ask for a list of his ancestors going back to 1750 and, of course, his medical report, in addition to the certificate from the Hitler Youth. Moreover, we require a certificate which makes clear that his family have no history of hereditary disease. Finally, we look at the report of the Racial Commission, consisting of Führer S.S. and some ethnologists and doctors. We do not only look at the height of the man or the colour of his eyes; we often reject men who are taller than 1 metre 80, even 1 metre 85, if their body-build is not good.

The starkness and beauty of a military liturgy, extended to perfection. The *Leibstandarte* marches past.

It is also important to see how the young man behaves in front of the Commission, how he holds his hands, whether he is disciplined, whether he has a servile manner, whether he is capable of replying freely and to the point, what sort of a bearing he has – in order to gauge whether he corresponds to our ideal. We had some difficulties with the Army, who could never understand the reasons for our rejecting certain candidates. But we remained intransigent on this point, and we did succeed in forming a real élite. Today (in 1937), the S.S. is organised in the following way: of the *Allgemeine S.S.* (General S.S.) – some 180,000 men – most are part-timers, who have outside jobs; they only become full-timers from the rank of *Sturmbannführer* (Major).

We are proud that only 0.4 % of our *Allgemeine S.S.* men have been recruited from the ranks of the unemployed. All our men are qualified

Nuremberg, September 1935 Congress. The *Allgemeine S.S.* marches past.

On the left, *Oberführer* (Lieutenant-General) in the uniform of 1938. He has the armband of a member of the *Reichsführer* S.S.'s Staff. On the right, *Sturmbannführer* (Major) of a *Reiterstandarte* (Cavalry Regiment). White summer uniform (1938).

From left to right: *Oberscharführer* (Sergeant-Major), drum major; *Untersturmführer* (Second Lieutenant), flagbearer; and *Brigadeführer* (Brigadier-General) wearing the sword and the embroidered belt (1938).

On the left: *Gefolgsmann* (Volunteer private) of the *Ehrhardt* Brigade, after it was absorbed by the S.S. in August 1933.

On the right: *Einheitsführer* (Captain) of the same Brigade.

at something. This is as it should be. A man should have his own value and get results in his job.

A man who changes his job for the third time without any particular reason does not interest us. We exclude him. We need keen men. The *Allgemeine S.S.* is, certainly, a civilian organisation, but it has to give its service even in the evenings and on Sundays, just as it did when we were still fighting for power. Along with it are the full-time units, the *S.S. Verfügungstruppe*, the *Totenkopfverbände*, the S.D. (Security Service) and *Rusha* (Service of Race and Population).

The men of the S.S. often live in localities or districts of towns which are far apart. In a town of 20 – 25,000 inhabitants, I cannot find enough suitable men to form a unit. So, we have a lot of formations in the countryside, meeting on Saturdays and Sundays.

From the age point of view, the S.S. is organised as follows: a young man of 18 is regarded as a junior; three years later, if he is selected, he swears an oath to the Führer and then becomes a probationer, in which capacity he has to reach a certain standard in sport; at 19 he enters the Labour Service, and finally goes into the Army.

Two years later, when he comes out of the Army – unless he stays in it as a non-commissioned officer or as an officer – he is still an S.S. probationer. Now comes his indoctrination with the ideology of the

Accompanied by *Gruppenführer* Sepp Dietrich, Hitler inspects a barrack room of the *Leibstandarte*.

Movement – in his first year at this stage he is given an elementary course in our concept of the world; he learns the laws governing marriage, legislation, family organisation and he also learns the rules of honour.

"On the 9th November which follows the termination of the tour of duty with the Wehrmacht, he becomes an S.S. soldier like the rest of us. Our rule is that the *Reichsführer S.S.* is an S.S. man by no more right than the ordinary S.S. private soldier. On this 9th November, therefore, he is handed a dagger and promises to observe correct conduct in marriage and family organisation and to respect S.S. laws. From this day on, he participates in the S.S. rights to defend personal honour by arms, rights which are not held by S.S. juniors and probationers. The S.S. man remains active in the *Allgemeine S.S.* up to the age of 35. Between 35 and 45 he forms part of the reserve and, when older, wears the grey badge of the veteran section. He has a lot of things to do between the age of 21 and 35 – especially up to 25 – e.g. route marching and taking part in sporting trials and military games of all sorts, designed to show up the best men, particularly on Summer Solstice Day, 21st June.

The S.S. men were forced to go in for sport. Every year, they had an assessment of their sporting prowess, to which Himmler himself was also subjected. We see here a football team.

Until he is 50, every S.S. man has to give annual proof of his standard in sport. We should bear in mind that nearly three-fifths of the S.S. are civilians, very involved with their normal jobs. They also suffer from the miserable living conditions in large towns – a great physical handicap; most people have forgotten how to walk; they prefer to take the underground, the railway or their own cars, and thus become pale and fat. For this reason I compel my S.S. men to go in for sport, and I inspect them every year. As Head of Police, I see large numbers of terrible examples of members of the German population who are dying of alcoholism. Though I would not exactly like to say to every S.S. man: 'Take up sport to stop drinking', it is a fact that games and sporting competitions do make you smoke and drink less. This is absolutely necessary, anyway, because otherwise good results cannot be achieved.

I have often discussed this question with the Hitler Youth. It is a vital matter that a generation shall live to grow old. In ancient times, the oldest men were the toughest. It is far from proven that men whose bodies are old are in any material sense "aged". The ancient Senates were institutions of psychological granite, which held firm to honour, even at the most critical moments. The Roman Senate was made up of extremely old men, but their minds were strong and active: when the Cimbri and the Teutoni sent delegates to demand land, while the young Romans were willing to give in, the Assembly of the Ancients refused to give any ground whatsoever. A people has to be nurtured for generations to reach old age with these powers intact, to ensure that men do not become prematurely enfeebled.

2. *The Concentration Camps*

"Talking of the *Totenkopfverbände* leads me on to the concentration camps. We have in Germany the following concentration camps: Dachau, Sachsenhausen, Lichtenburg, Sachsenburg and a few smaller ones. We shall be having more. The number of internees was 8000 in 1937. I would like to explain to you why we have as many as we have, and why we are going to have more. The reasons are these.

The Communist Party is well organised. Part of its permanent force is abroad; the others have been arrested and are now in the concentration camps, since we reason that the mass of workers in this country will readily back our Party provided that the representatives of other ideologies don't indoctrinate them with other ideas. It is obvious that a man who has been known as a Communist for years holds Communist beliefs. Some of the permanent Communists still at large went to Russia, where they were given special courses teaching them new tactics. They got false passports directly from the Ogpu. They then came back to Germany and set up in regions where they were not known. It has been very difficult to root them out.

When I took over the command of the Gestapo in 1934, I did not publish anything about the illegal Communist Party because I considered that the activities of the police should be performed in

S.S. Totenkopfverbände – the S.S. unit with the Death's Head badge.

Lapel insignia (worn on the right) of members of the staff at Dachau.

"Shop closed by the police for exorbitant pricing. The proprietor has been put into protective custody at Dachau. Head of Political Section of the Bavarian Police. Signed: Himmler".

silence. By 1936 we had liquidated on two occasions the leaders of the German Communist Party, but you did not read anything of that in your papers. However, the activity of that Party remains considerable: on the one hand, the Comintern has plenty of money and, on the other hand, the Ogpu has a budget for its subversive activities of 1,300,000,000 Marks. We are surrounded by countries which turn a blind eye to Communist activities, and this makes our situation very difficult. That is why, with the Fuhrer's agreement, I started interning hard-line Communists, so that we could all sleep more easily in our beds. We're going to increase the number of internees more and more, so that we shall make it impossible for any illegal organisation to be created, because there will not be enough people to do so.

I would not have you in any doubt that nobody is unjustly interned in these camps. You find there the cess-pit of criminal scum. They are all syphilitic ne'er-do-wells. You cannot find any more vivid demonstration of the correctness of the hereditary and racial laws than in any concentration camp. There you will see people who are brain-damaged, who squint, who have deformed bodies, half-Jews, in general a large number of persons who are inferior from a racial point of view. We naturally make a distinction among the internees between those

"Education is possible thanks to the order that we maintain in the camps: H. Himmler".

Himmler visits the concentration camp at Dachau in 1935. Behind him comes Victor Lutze, who had succeeded Röhm at the Head of the S.A.

whom we are keeping for some months in order to educate them and those who will have to stay for a very long time.

Education is carried out by the order that we cause to reign in the camps. It is never carried out by incarnating any concept of the world at all, for these internees have, for the most part, slavish minds, very few have any real character at all. Their slavish minds would make them agree to anything you asked of them. They would repeat in parrot fashion everything that is written in the *Völkischer Beobachter* (the Party organ), but they would always remain the same in reality.

Education is carried out by the order in which the internees must live, a strict order and a severe discipline. The order consists in making them live in clean huts. No other people but the Germans would do so much for them; no other people would be human enough. Their body linen is changed frequently. They have to wash twice a day. In one camp, we have professional miscreants: 500 men, each of which has been condemned to eight or ten years imprisonment. Some of them have been condemned thirty times. I visit every camp once a year, and I always go unannounced. I recently met a man of 72 who had committed his 63rd crime. It would be an insult to animals to treat a man of this nature like an animal. No animal would behave in this way. I intend to intern all professional criminals after their third or fourth offence. There is no reason why they should be allowed to go free, the more so as it costs a lot of money to keep track of them.

The camps are surrounded with electric wires. If anyone goes into the prohibited zone, he is shot at; if anyone takes to his heels while at work, he is similarly shot at. If anyone is awkward, he is put into isolation in a dark cell, his nourishment is restricted to bread and water and, according to Prussian law, he may receive up to 25 strokes with a cane. There is nothing brutal about this punishment, because it can only be awarded by the inspector for concentration camps."

Untersturmführer (Second Lieutenant) – on the left; *Oberscharführer* (Sergeant-Major) – on the right; both belong to the S.D.

3. Missions of the Security Service

"I now come to the Security Service (S.D.). This Service became the main source of information, in respect of our concept of the world, for both the Party and, finally, for the State too. At the beginning, at the time when we were still fighting, it was only the S.S.'s information service – it is the principle of the S.S. not to be interested in day-to-day problems.

Politics is of interest to us only as a function of the decades and centuries to come. In consequence, we free our men from daily cares; they know they are serving a cause of a nature that recurs only once in two thousand years.

The S.D. is made up of 3–4000 men and its influence extends to Communism, the Jews, Freemasonry, Ultramontanism, the political activity of the religious sects and the forces of reaction generally. The executive of the S.D. is not concerned with detailed problems, only with ideological problems.

Here's an example. Let us suppose that the Ultramontanes (supporters of a party believing in the Pope's temporal domination) draw up a scientific synthesis of the Austrians, which might in the end transform Austria into a sort of Switzerland, in the attempt to drive it out of the German community. This matter would be of interest to the S.D. The S.D. would then look into the matter of the German professors who were dealing with this project and would question their contacts with bodies abroad. The S.D. is not interested in the Communist Party's cells – that is the concern of the police executive – but it is interested in the influence of Bolshevism on Masonic circles abroad and in the encounters the principal emissaries have. For example, 800 delegates recently met in Austria. The S.D. naturally asked what plans they had for Germany. Where is their attack going to be made? On the atheist front or on the religious front – backing up the priests? What economic influence do the Jews exert in acts of sabotage and the black market in currency? These are things that the S.D. has studied. They call for work extending sometimes over many years.

We are all the time preoccupied by questions of internal security. But we must realise that the enemy is not merely a foe, in a military sense, but that he is also an ideological enemy. When I speak of a foe I mean our natural enemy, Jewish/Freemasonic Bolshevism; its capital may be in Russia, but this does not mean that the threat of a Bolshevik attack

The insignia of the *Sicherheitsdienst*, (the Security Service).

"The most important thing is to ensure that our ideological concept enters into the minds of the whole of our people". *Himmler*.

has to come from Russia. States and peoples led by Jewish/Bolshevik coteries, or which are influenced by them, will always be our enemies and will always constitute a danger for us. At the same time, we must realise that Bolshevism is an organisation of sub-men, entirely dominated by Judaism, and that it represents, in consequence, the precise opposite of what an Aryan people loves and appreciates. It is a doctrine which appeals to the lowest instincts of man and which makes a religion of them.

Bolshevism, with its Lenin conserved in the Kremlin, will only need another score of years to become a religion centred in Asia, designed to destroy the whole white world. Bolshevism methodically works to

The Grand Inquisitor and his "Shadow".

13th March 1938 – One People, one Reich, one Führer.

bolshevise other peoples and destroy white men. One of its first acts, dictated by its Jewish leaders in 1918, was to set up an Asiatic university, with departments for each Asiatic people, to study local languages, customs, religious problems and economies. The students at this university were then sent into the heartlands of the respective peoples as residents, to study their needs, religions, fanaticism and social difficulties. Their aim was to persuade the people that only the men of Moscow can help them. The whole of this movement is above all directed against the white man, especially against the awakened Germany, which had long been thought to be dead and buried.

If we wish to remain immune against this poison, we must have social prosperity and law and order as our base. But the most important thing is to ensure that our ideological concepts deeply penetrate the whole of our people. This minority of 70 million men in the centre of Europe can only exist because we are qualitatively better than the others. We are better than the others, who are more numerous than we and who will ever remain so. We are superior in value, because this is inherent in the quality of our blood. Our blood is more inventive than that of others, and it allows us to lead our people better, to make better soldiers of them, to have better statesmen and to reach a higher state of culture. We shall retain this value as long as we keep our people in good health, as long as this people admits and applies the old laws of conservation which National Socialism, thanks to Adolf Hitler, has restored to us.

We shall remain healthy and strong to resist as long as we do not fall into the slough of democracy or into the nefarious regime of an hereditary monarchy, which does not come from the people themselves. Let us be quite clear about this: we shall not exist for years and centuries to come unless we have confidence in our own strength alone and unless we are resolute to maintain it.

I have been talking about the penetration of our ideological concepts into our people, in case of war. If this war were to arrive earlier than we predict or than we desire, we must not hide from ourselves that there will always be, within the German people, a certain amount of ground which is fertile for the Comintern. The latter's task is easy, for the Comintern is, at one and the same time, an organisation of political agitators and military spies. Every Communist is a military spy: based on his belief that his imaginary homeland is in Moscow, he will deliver up every secret of production and every military secret; he will act and destroy by his political ideology in order to provoke revolution. The danger will be greater if war comes earlier. We must reckon with having to take part in this theatre of internal war and we must realise that a war will be lost if we neglect the internal front.

The intelligence of this internal war theatre must be all round us. It signifies the 'to be or not to be!' of our German people when the hour of trial comes. This question of internal security must be resolved positively with the aid of the S.S. and the police. That is our Führer's order. We shall execute it with all seriousness, for we are truly convinced that this is no work of secondary importance. Only the ideological education of our men and the establishment of a racial elite will enable us to confront the problem."

CHAPTER 4

The Empire of the Black Prince

The tentacles of the S.S.

Tired of the disorders of the Weimar Republic, the Germans saw reborn in the S.S. the traditional order and discipline which was so dear to their hearts. The theme of the élite found an immense amount of approbation. A new wave of recruits brought into the S.S. a considerable contingent from the aristocracy. They thought they would see in the S.S. the qualities that they used to love in the Kaiser's army. Among them some of the most respected names from the Prussian aristocracy, notably the Prince of Hohenzollern-Emden, the Count von der Schulenburg, the Duke of Mecklenburg and the Prince of Waldeck-Pyrmont.

While intensifying his recruitment, Himmler continued to respect his principle of a permanent purging process, aimed at excluding notorious opportunists, alcoholics, homosexuals, men whose Aryan descent was dubious, the ruffians of the early days and the unemployable. This process of selection attracted all those who thought they belonged to the élite, above all the nobles who were disgusted by the Republic and ruined by the defeat of 1918 and the consequent economic crisis. Even if the old Junkers frowned on the new Order, insisting that it was only made up of a band of parvenus, their sons, on the other hand, were far more forthcoming; by the end of 1934, Hitler was able to welcome into the ranks of the S.S. the whole of the young Prussian aristocracy.

Gorget of the S.S. Military Police. A patrol was made up of two men and a non-commissioned officer. They were responsible for checking the correct conduct of the men of the S.S. in public. The plate was of nickel (1936).

A number of intellectuals also joined the S.S., attracted by the success of the new formation. By so doing, they were able to make a career without having to show evidence of having belonged to the Party for years. These young intellectuals, including a number of jurists, hoped to find in the S.S. a future to satisfy their ambitions. Heydrich was their leader, and it was he who attracted them to the S.D. They were to transform this political police service into the most technically advanced arm of the S.S.

A different group of intellectuals, with a more scientific bent, joined the S.S. at the same time. Although their accession did not create as much stir as the Heydrich group, their efficiency in their own sphere was considerable. They were to form the framework of the economic projects of the S.S., constituting a vast area of the scientific coverage of the Black Order.

Once the War had come, the S.S. gradually took control of trading companies they had confiscated from enemies of the regime. This role of the S.S. is very little known. While, of course, we think of the mineral water factory of Mattoni, the porcelain factory of Allach or the Norland publications, it is easy to forget that the S.S. exploited the mines and mills in which the K.S. Oswald Pohl (Oswald Pohl Concentration Camp) inmates worked. Pohl was head of the W.V.H.A., responsible for the general administration of the concentration camps, but he was also responsible for the management and administration of the S.S. trading companies. He was a superior technician, of a similar type to Heydrich, and his main aim was to obtain a high output of work. This often brought him into conflict with the Gestapo; for him, the camps were primarily a source of labour, but for the Secret Police the aim of the camps lay in their repressive function. These two concepts of the concentration camps were to coexist to the end of the War.

Pohl controlled the Waffen S.S.'s administration and accounts. He supervised the twenty concentration camps and the hundred and sixty work camps, as also the S.S. workshops and factories. He grouped together all these various undertakings (quarries, mines, food, textile and leather factories) into a single trust, the D.W.B. (*Deutsche Wirtschaftsbetriebe* = German Economic Undertakings), which was to practise a systematic policy of buying up competitors – in the best capitalist tradition.

Pohl was later to control more or less 75% of the German mineral water market, practically the whole of the German and Czechoslovak production of furniture and all the building material factories within the occupied territories of the East (*Ostdeutsche Baustoffwerke GmbH* = East German Building Materials Works). He was also to have a finger in the pie of a number of printing houses.

Obergruppenführer (Lieutenant-General) Oswald Pohl, head of the W.V.H.A., responsible for the S.S.'s economic activities, including responsibility for the administration of the concentration camps; a cold, efficient and unfeeling technocrat.

Pohl's adjutant, the engineer Kammler, was to create an autonomous armaments industry for the purposes of the Waffen S.S. It was Kammler who later built Hitler's underground headquarters in Thuringia and a number of underground aeronautical factories. It was he who developed the M.E. 262 jet fighters and, in collaboration with S.S. Führer Wernher von Braun, he was to bring out the V1 and V2 missiles. It was because of the part he played in the construction and

A gigantic and pitiless utilisation of slave labour in the service of the war economy of the Reich. Here we see the quarries at Matthausen.

launching of these secret weapons that he was placed in 1944 under Hitler's direct orders, a striking confirmation of the technical levels the S.S. had reached.

The Black Order also attracted military men. Some officers were attracted by the almost experimental modernity of the S.S. and left the *Reichswehr* to join the Black Order. However, the *Reichswehr* (known as the Wehrmacht from 1935 onwards) looked with a very jaundiced eye on this poaching, and the S.S. was prohibited from recruiting career officers. *Obergruppenführer* (Lieutenant-General) Gottlob Berger, whom Hitler put at the head of the S.S.H.A., the controlling authority of the S.S., making him responsible for its general management

The Duke of Windsor reviewed the *Germania* Regiment, one of the first units of the *S.S. Verfügungstruppe*, the future Waffen S.S., on 13th October 1937 at the Ordensburg of Grossinsee.

(administration, recruitment and ideology), was at all times a prey to endless difficulties as long as he was recruiting sergeant for the S.S. However he, like others, was fully equal to his daunting task, which included the enormous extension of the Waffen S.S. during the War.

The future Waffen S.S. existed in embryo as early as 1933, when the *Leibstandarte S.S. Adolf Hitler* and the *Totenkopfverbände* were set up, but Himmler's aims went much further: the S.S. was destined to become the crucible of a new army. He had no confidence whatsoever in the old *Reichswehr*. He took a new step on 24th September 1934 by setting up the *S.S. Verfügungstruppe* to recruit career officers who were weary of the inactivity and rigid character of the *Reichswehr*. They included General Paul Hausser and Major Felix Steiner.

As early as 1934, Himmler set up a *Junker* School at Brunswick to train the S.S. cadets. However, the S.S., the sole criterion of which was personal worth, was not recognised by the General Staff. Whereas the generals belonged to an age-old military caste, the S.S. represented for them a gang of military parvenus, policemen rather than soldiers. This scorn and hostility was never cancelled out, even when the Waffen S.S. had proved itself in the field. It was not until the 2nd March 1940, after the Polish Campaign, that the name of Waffen S.S. was made official.

In the meantime, the generals refused to confer any military status on the *S.S. Verfügungstruppe*. Relying on the principle that they alone had the monopoly of armed force, as recognised by the law, they resisted Hitler point blank and refused to provide weapons to the S.S. regiments. The hostility was open for all to see. The S.S. countermeasure was not long in coming.

Thanks to its remarkable information service, the S.D. was to break the careers of the two highest dignitaries of the Wehrmacht's General Staff, Marshal von Blomberg and General von Fritsch. Von Blomberg had one weak point – women. He liked them and they liked him. Perhaps he was not sufficiently discreet in his choice of liaisons. On 12th January 1938, he married a young woman who, unfortunately, had a police record. During the General's honeymoon, the S.D. sent the Count von Helldorf, Chief of Police, a thick and highly compromising file about the new Frau von Blomberg, an ex-callgirl. Helldorf sent the file on to General Keitel, Blomberg's adjutant and friend. Keitel ducked the responsibility, and advised Helldorf to let Goering know about the matter. Once Goering had the file in his hands, he promptly alerted the Führer. The latter's reaction was predictable:

he decided that Blomberg would have to resign when he returned from his honeymoon and be asked to go abroad so that his name would be forgotten.

It was far more difficult to throw discredit on General von Fritsch, because he was very popular with the Army. However, the S.D. found a file concerning homosexuality, which might possibly concern von Fritsch. They managed to find a witness, who was being held by the Gestapo. Heydrich constructed a case, which he thought was cast-iron, on the basis of these few vague presumptions, but at first Hitler refused to be convinced. Heydrich came back to the charges in 1938, and this time, although the file was still pretty thin, Hitler looked at it with more attention. He still had great difficulty in believing this story, so Himmler advised him to confront the witness and von Fritsch. This confrontation took place on 24th January 1938. General von Fritsch was called into the Führer's presence, and came into the office where Goering, Himmler and Heydrich were already assembled. Without saying a word, Hitler opened a second door, and a young man came in the room, looked at the General and shouted: "That's him; I can recognise him."

Thunderstruck, Fritsch flushed to the roots of his hair and showed how shaken he was, like a schoolboy brought before his headmaster for punishment. Hardly had he pulled himself together than Hitler, without

Marshal von Blomberg and General von Fritsch in conversation with Hitler. Leaders of the Wehrmacht, they represented the old military caste which was hostile to Nazism. They were eliminated, thanks to the machinations of the S.D.

The Black Army was able to organise itself properly after Marshal Blomberg and General Fritsch had been eliminated.

listening to his protestations, issued the order that he be suspended for "health reasons". Fritsch was quite determined he was not going to leave matters there. He obtained signatures to a petition from several generals and was successful in winning the right to appear before a military tribunal in order to clear his name. The hearing exonerated him and decided that a mistake had been made, if not an actual police frame up. Hitler overwhelmed Fritsch with praise, but he never gave him back his old job. On 4th February, Hitler took personal command of the whole of the armed forces. There was now no barrier left between the Wehrmacht and the National Socialist power.

Both aristocrats and peasants managed to find a place in the S.S. To this extent, it perfectly fulfilled the mission it had set for itself, in wishing to set up an élite based on quality and not on birth. Nevertheless, each social group fulfilled in the S.S. different functions: statistics show that, in the beginning at least, the members of the middle class did not particularly care for the *Verfügungstruppe*; they more naturally went in for administrative pursuits, in which they excelled.

The men of finance and industry also had the opportunity of joining the S.S. For them, the *Freundeskreis Heinrich Himmler* (Circle of Friends of Heinrich Himmler) was set up. Among the initiates, this Circle was called the *Kepplerkreis* (the Keppler Circle), named after its founder, Wilhelm Keppler. It was made up of associated benefactor members, the so-called *fördernde mitglieder* (supporter members). These gave considerable financial assistance in the form of donations to the cultural and social work of the *Reichsführer S.S.* The Secretary of the Circle, the great industrialist and *S.S. Obersturmführer* (Lieutenant)

Fritz Kranefuss, was commissioned by Himmler to collect the funds. In July 1936, Himmler invited the members of the Circle to the ceremony organised to celebrate the anniversary of the death of Henry the Fowler (King of Germany from 919 to 936) at Quedlinburg. But Himmler finally lost interest in the Circle and instructed the Secretary to seize the funds – the members of the Circle were making fun of the ideology of the S.S. and only joining to attract Himmler's favour and protection. Their keen calculations only partially achieved their aims and deceived nobody. When, in 1937, Dr. Eugen Vögler, the Managing Director of I.G. Farben, showed himself particularly generous in order to get into the *Freundeskreis*, Kranefuss was to remark cynically: "Herr Vögler is no idealist. He's not even the head of a company such as the S.S. would wish. His donation will only be accepted to the extent that it does not put the S.S. under an obligation. However, it will have the effect that Herr Vögler will be able to boast about his good relations with the S.S."

After the industrialists, most of the banks and big companies were to see their directors enter the S.S. as *fördernde mitglieder*. Supporter Members received, in exchange for the sums they poured out, a medal struck with the swastika and the initials F.M. They were also given an S.S. calendar, published by Nordland. They even had their own periodical, to keep them informed about the S.S. activities and to recall to them the principles by which they were theoretically bound: "It is an

Before the tomb of King Henry I the Fowler at Quedlinburg and in the presence of the honorary and benefactor members of the S.S., Himmler takes the vow to be faithful to the example of the Germanic King.

honour to belong to the S.S. It is an honour to be an Associate Member of the S.S. Let each one do his duty. We, the S.S., and you, the Associate Members of the S.S., all have our places. Germany will once more become great."

Himmler also created another form of membership, which induced numbers of writers, scientists and leading civil servants to put on the elegant black uniform. He gave them the honorary title of *S.S. Ehrenführer* (S.S. Honorary Leader).

As its activities became more and more numerous and diversified, the S.S. tended to become a state within a state, particularly when it was at the height of its power in 1943. At the geographical level, this year saw the greatest expansion of the S.S. Himmler still at this stage controlled all services, the activity of which was perfectly co-ordinated. With its organisation represented in all the Germanic countries, and in the occupied countries as well, the S.S. was at the spearhead of the administration of the Reich. No other service attained its scope and efficiency.

The Waffen S.S. raised volunteers in all countries and was represented on all the fields of battle. The *Ahnenerbe* (Heritage of the Ancestors) had ramifications extending to the Caucasus, and the R.S.H.A. (National Security Centre) had sections in all the occupied countries and agents in the others. The *Napolas* (National Education Establishments) were schools both within and outside the Reich, sending their pupils for courses of study to Africa and America. The S.S. became a formidable organisation, comprising institutes of scientific and cultural research – such as the *Ahnenerbe* – as well as armed forces. It had an enormous potential of cheap labour to draw upon in the concentration camps. It was capable of living off its own resources, since it formed its own cadet forces, thanks to the *Napolas* and its connections with the University. It also had the best information service in Germany. It had a co-ordination and a centralisation which were more efficient than the other departments of the Reich.

The S.S.'s most surprising enterprise was, without any doubt, its newspaper, the *Schwarzes Korps* (the Black Corps), set up in 1935 on Heydrich's initiative and directed by Gunther d'Alquen. During the War, circulation reached 750,000 copies. The reasons for this success are curious: the *Schwarzes Korps* was the only organ of the entire German press which was not censored and, although it was rigorously orthodox at the ideological level, it was also the only paper that gave any

Gunther d'Alquen, S.S. *Sturmbannführer* (Major), the non-conformist director of the *Schwarzes Korps*.

indication of having critical and non-conformist spirit, whilst still remaining closely bound to one of the motive forces of the Reich.

From its very first number, the originality of the new weekly was emphasized by its aggressiveness to the rest of the Press, censored by Goebbels. In the conflict between Italy and Abyssinia, it adopted an attitude that was frankly anti-Italian at a time when the Press as a whole was supporting the Italians. *Schwarzes Korps* took sides against the tyranny of the leaders of the Party, attacked the bourgeois ministers and denounced the inadequacies of the Administration in the words: "A Party card is not a ration card: we shall not prove our loyalty to the Führer by having his portrait on our teacups or the swastika at the bottom of our tankards of beer. People cannot live on slogans and words. History is written by those who act, not those who talk."

Of all the subordinate activities of the S.S., it was the police organisation which was to leave the most terrifying memory, but also the most frightening example of efficiency.

When the Gestapo was set up in 1933, it had 35 members – a number which reached 607 by 1935. Whereas its expenses amounted to a million Marks in 1933, the figure was 40 million in 1935. For its part, on the other hand, the S.D. had 3000 active members in 1937 and 50,000 more or less well-disposed informers, responsible for gathering information on everything and everybody. Thus, the enemies of the regime were card-indexed and categorised, from the Jehovah's Witnesses to the fanatical anti-Nazis. As the computer was not yet invented, coloured cards were used with pegs; the colour of the card or peg rapidly informed the S.D. of the category of the person in whom they were interested. Thus, at the slightest whisper of suspicion, the S.D. was able to pick out dubious or dangerous persons.

The enemies of the regime were divided into three groups:

Group A1: Enemies of the regime to be imprisoned in case of a probable mobilisation; the card was distinguished by a red peg in the left hand margin.
Group A2: Enemies of the regime to be imprisoned in case of certain mobilisation; a blue peg.
Group A3: Citizens who did not, properly speaking, endanger the State, but who, to use Heydrich's words, deserved to be closely supervised, or even to be arrested in time of war, by reason of their political apathy; a green peg.

A second peg in the right hand margin of the card defined the nature of the enemy: a red peg signified a Communist, a pink peg a Marxist, a brown peg a saboteur and a violet peg a critic.

The card index was brought up to date in respect of every card twice a year (on 1st April and 1st October).

The headquarters of the Gestapo at Berlin, 8 Prinz-Albert-Strasse.

The General Staff of the Security Police. From left to right: Huber, Nebe, Himmler, Heydrich and Müller (*Ullstein*).

The power of the new police force came into momentary conflict with the ambitions of the Minister of the Interior, Dr. Frick. He tried to regain the advantage and to bring all the police forces of the Reich under the aegis of the Ministry of the Interior. For this purpose, he tried to get the support of *S.S. Gruppenführer* Daluege against Himmler – the latter was to be given honorary functions, while Daluege would be put at the effective head of the command posts. Neither Himmler nor Heydrich, however, would look at it in this way. On 9th June 1936, Heydrich asked Hitler to give the *Reichsführer S.S.* the rank of Minister and the title: "*Reichsführer S.S.* and Head of the German Police". Himmler did not, in fact, yet receive the rank of Minister, but he nevertheless installed himself at the Ministry of Interior on 17th June to supervise the Police Department. Hitler specified that "the Minister may ask him (Himmler) to give an account of his activities, exclusively at a personal level and without the presence of any intermediary." This meant that the administrative supervision of the Minister over the Police Department was purely fictional. Dr. Frick had to bow before the storm. As soon as Himmler had taken up his post, he re-organised the Ministry services. The police force henceforth comprised two large structural organisations, as follows.

On the one hand, the *Sicherheitspolizei (Sipo)* (Security Police) brought together the civil services – the Gestapo (Political Police) and the *Kripo* (Criminal Police); it was controlled by Heydrich, who also kept in his own hands the S.D., a service which properly belonged to the S.S. On the other hand, the *Ordnungspolizei (Orpo)* (Public Order Police) brought together the police forces in uniform – the *Schutzpolizei (Schupo)* (Protection Police), comprising the constabulary in both town and country districts; the *Orpo* was put in the hands of *Obergruppenführer S.S.* and General of Police Kurt Daluege.

The S.S. had, thus, won a new round, largely thanks to the capable administration of the S.D. and the services rendered by Heydrich, that is to say, thanks to the influx of intellectuals, who had given the S.D., and even the S.S., their genius for organisation and their flair for administration. Heydrich commissioned one of the most brilliant of these, Walter Schellenberg, to work out a project to fuse the S.D. which was a Party organisation, with the *Sipo*, (on which the Gestapo depended), a State organisation, making of the combination an organisation to be known as *Reichssicherheitshauptampt* (R.S.H.A.) – the National Security Central Office. A project of this nature did not appeal to everybody; it particularly failed to do so in the case of Werner

Walter Schellenberg, one of Heydrich's most brilliant protégés. He was Director of S.D.-Ausland (the foreign espionage service) from 1941 onwards.

Heinrich Müller, policeman by profession, who joined the National Socialist movement rather late for opportunist reasons. Head of the Gestapo. He disappeared in 1945.

Best, the boss of the Gestapo, who was very keen on maintaining the distinction between State and Party.

Nevertheless, the R.S.H.A. did see the light of day in September 1939, based on a compromise according to which certain of its sections were placed under the authority of the Party and others under the authority of the State. In fact, this distinction became more and more obscured, especially following the resignation in May 1940 of Werner Best. Although the R.S.H.A. was officially subordinate to Himmler, since he was Supreme Commander of the S.S. at the same time as Minister of the Interior, it quickly became Heydrich's empire.

Dr. Werner Best, disciple of Ernst Jünger and an admirer of Hitler. He was one of the organisers of the R.S.H.A., but resigned in 1940 because he was opposed to the War.

S.S. Gruppenführer (Major-General) Otto Ohlendorf and Heinz Jost. The former was in charge of the S.D.-Inland (internal affairs – political information and counter espionage) and the latter of S.D.-Ausland (espionage) until 1941. Both of these officers were in command of *Einsatzgruppen* (Task Forces) in the East.

The R.S.H.A. was divided into seven main sections, called *Ämter* (Departments):

Amt I: Personnel: for the whole of the R.S.H.A. This Department was led by Werner Best until 1940 – a senior civil servant and a jurist, who thought he saw in Hitler the reincarnation of Law. At the start of the War, however, he found himself opposed to the new tendencies in National Socialism. He was succeeded by men of smaller stature, Streckenbach, Schulze and Ehrlinger.
Amt II: *Haushalt und Wirtschaft* (Home and the Economy). Werner Best was the head of this Department also; he was followed, later, by Nockemann, Siegert and Spacil.
Amt III: *S.D.-Inland* (S.D. Internal). This was an information service, covering Germany and the associated countries. It was led by *S.S. Brigadeführer* (Brigadier) – later *S.S. Gruppenführer* (Major General) – Ohlendorf. At Nuremberg, Ohlendorf was the representative of the young S.S. intellectuals who scorned the mystique of the old Hitlerians and considered themselves to be the true trustees of National Socialism.
Amt IV: Gestapo (State Secret Police). This Department was directed by Heinrich Müller. The post carried the right to make arrests

in political matters and to decide who was to be interned in concentration camps. His task was the struggle against the enemies of the regime. The Gestapo was itself divided into six groups, which were then divided into sub-groups. For example, group IV B 4 was led by Adolf Eichmann and was competent in Jewish matters. Group IV D 4 was responsible for the occupied territories of the West (France, Belgium and Holland) and was led by Karl Heinz Hoffmann.

Amt V: *Kriminelpolizei* or *Kripo* (Criminal Police). This active Department had executive powers in common-law crime. It was led by Arthur Nebe, who was later hanged in 1945 for his participation in the plot of 20th July against Hitler. He was replaced by Ranzinger.

Amt VI: *S.D.-Ausland* (S.D. External). This information service, directed against countries abroad, was successively led by Heinz Jost, and then, from 1941 onwards, by Walter Schellenberg. Schellenberg was, in many respects, one of the most interesting leaders within the framework of the R.S.H.A. He had been a pupil of the Jesuits and had read law and medicine before being attracted to the S.D. by Heydrich. He was one of the group of S.S. technocrats, who were totally without fanaticism and were above all concerned with efficiency. It was he who conducted preliminary peace negotiations with Count Bernadotte at the end of the War.

Amt VII: Ideological research and documentation. This

Dr. Ernst Kaltenbrunner, *Obergruppenführer* (Lieutenant-General) S.S., head of the R.S.H.A. (National Security Central Office) on Heydrich's death. He was an Austrian, who entered the S.S. clandestinely before the Anschluss. He was a fanatical National Socialist, faithful to the end.

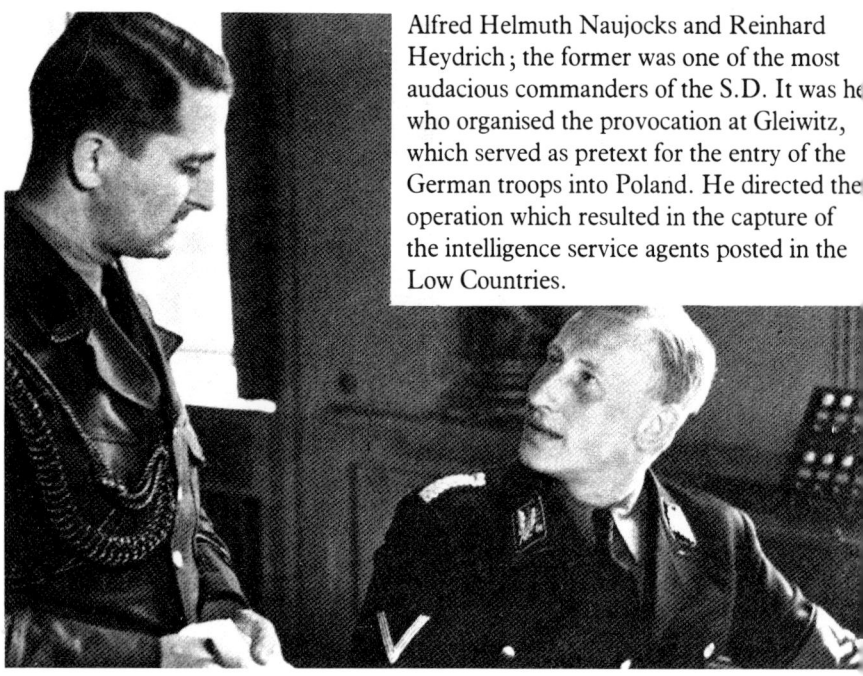

Alfred Helmuth Naujocks and Reinhard Heydrich; the former was one of the most audacious commanders of the S.D. It was he who organised the provocation at Gleiwitz, which served as pretext for the entry of the German troops into Poland. He directed the operation which resulted in the capture of the intelligence service agents posted in the Low Countries.

Department was led by Dittel and was primarily responsible for sounding public opinion.

The personnel of the R.S.H.A. was totally integrated into the S.S., but all members had the distinctive S.D. emblem.

The activities of the S.D., in particular, were extremely varied. They ranged from defamation of Soviet generals (for example, in the Tukachevsky affair) to the liberation of Mussolini by Skorzeny's commandos, or from frontier operations to the support given to German minorities in the different territories claimed by the Reich before the War. This is why the action which led up to the Anschluss in Austria was animated by the S.D.

As early as 1930, the S.S. Frauenfeld introduced black uniforms into Austria. It recruited and equipped assault squads. Later, the S.D. was responsible for infiltrating the Austrian police. German officers entered Austria secretly to conduct a campaign of intimidation, bomb attacks, telephone wire cutting, frontier skirmishes, setting up an Austrian Legion controlled by the S.S. and so on. In spite of the suppression of the S.A. and the S.S. in Austria and the closure of the Brown Houses, the Austrian Nazi organisation was never dismantled. Its spearhead was the *S.S. Standarte 89*, a clandestine unit, meeting under the cover of an athletic association. 154 of its men took part in the attack on Chancellor Dollfuss on 25th July 1934. The successor to Dollfuss, Schuschnigg, concluded an agreement with the Führer which, in its secret clauses, permitted the setting-up of Nazi organisations in Austria.

From then on, the cries of *Sieg Heil* and *Heil Hitler*, as also the songs *Horst Wessel Lied* and *Deutschland über Alles* resounded through the streets of Vienna. During all this time, the S.S. and S.A. services were infiltrating the Army. However, it was not in Vienna that the S.S. did most of its recruiting, but in the more outright German provinces – especially Tyrol. As soon as an organisation was dissolved,

The Austrian Legion, set up by the S.S. on German territory with Nazi militants who had been expelled from Austria.

Photograph taken before Austria became part of Germany: The grandfather's notice says "To think that we've lived to see this"; and the girl's notice "When shall I see the Führer?"

it was immediately re-created under a new name. Thus, the S.S. took the anodyne name of "Special Duties" and the Hitler Youth became the "Austrian National Socialist Youth". The headquarters of these formations was at Judenburg, near Graz. In the evening, after dark, 5000 S.A. would march in tight formation through the streets, taking up the whole carriageway. The S.S. police would direct the traffic and the pedestrians. From rank to rank rang out the song:

> *Heute gehört uns Deutschland*
> *Morgen schon die ganze Welt.*
> To-day Germany belongs to us
> Tomorrow the rest of the world.

Dr. Seyss-Inquart, the leader of the Austrian Nazis, saluted the crowd whilst the *Horst Wessel Lied* was sung. A body of picked men marched down the street. They did not yet wear uniform. They would join the S.S. after the *Anschluss* (the Union with Austria).

In Vienna, both the S.A. and S.S. were moving about the streets already. On the eve of the plebiscite, eight hundred of them took up their positions in front of the Chancellery. As soon as the results were announced, the S.S. moved in on the premises of the assault police. The S.D. and the Gestapo were in their places too.

The same method was used in Czechoslovakia. Here, the S.D. relied on the Sudeten German minority, led by Dr. Henlein. The Sudetens were the largest minority in Czechoslovakia, so that Hitler could easily invoke in their favour the right of all peoples to arrange their own lives. These three thousand six hundred Germans lived, for the most part, in the so-called Sudetenland, which formed a crescent around Bohemia and Moravia. To back this movement for the return of his people to Germany, Dr. Henlein set up a German patriotic front, the *Deutsche Heimatfront* (German Homeland Front), on 1st October 1934. By 1935, the Henlein group had won sufficient support to become a real party. It changed its name and became the *Sudetendeutsche Partei* (S.D.P.). The new party received funds from the V.O.M.I. (the organisation of Germans living abroad), directed by S.S. Obergruppenführer (Lieutenant-General) Lorenz. By 1938, S.D. agents were already at work; they infiltrated into all sorts of associations, for example, cultural and sporting clubs. The regional veterans' associations brought the S.D. such a flood of information that special telephone lines had to be installed at the frontier to communicate directly with Berlin. Just as the S.D. had assembled an Austrian Legion on the Austrian frontier, made up of political refugees, it organised a Sudeten German volunteer corps on the Czechoslovak frontier. The headquarters of this formation was in Bayreuth, in the castle at Donndorf.

Dr. Seyss-Inquart, leader of the Austrian Nazis, in his uniform as *S.S. Gruppenführer* (Major-General). On his left, we see Hitler, and on Hitler's left *Gauleiter* (Regional Leader) Bürkel, who was stationed in Vienna after the *Anschluss*.

Demonstration in support of the Sudeten German minorities.

Hitler decided to go into action in September 1938. On the 19th of that month the Volunteer Corps penetrated Czechoslovakia clandestinely in commando squads of twelve men each. It was to carry out more than three hundred sorties and take more than fifteen hundred prisoners from the Czechoslovak forces. But hostilities ceased before they were properly started, because the Munich Conference opened on 29th September. The following day, it was decided that the Sudetenland would be officially handed over to Germany between 1st and 10th October.

By the Munich Agreement, the Sudeten Volunteer Corps officially passed into S.S. control, and was allocated to police functions. The complete occupation of Czechoslovakia was prepared by the S.D., relying on the Slovakian minority this time, since they were claiming autonomy from the Czechs. The Sudeten students from Bohemia and Moravia, incorporated in the S.S. and S.D., played a considerable part in infiltrating organisations of every type and by 15th March 1939, when the German troops penetrated the rest of Czechoslovakia, the country was already paralysed. The S.D. and Gestapo had a number of key contacts in the administration and police. The members of the

S.S. Leibstandarte and militant Sudeten Nazis.

student groups who had helped the S.D. were integrated into the S.S. Himmler accompanied Hitler into Prague on 15th March along with Heydrich, the future Protector of Bohemia/Moravia, and waxed most enthusiastic over the physical qualities of the Czech police, who were more or less agents of the S.D. He decided forthwith to incorporate them into the S.S. Henlein's Adjutant, Karl Hermann Frank, was put at the head of this police force and appointed *Gruppenführer S.S.* (Major-General) as a reward for services rendered.

The world well knows of the fate of the Jews in occupied Europe. In the absence of precise statistics, it is very difficult to quote exact figures. The number of Jews who perished as victims of the Nazis (in death camps, through the destruction of the ghetto at Warsaw, during the exodus from Russia, in mass executions, ill-treatment and acts of war in general) varies from 1,100,000 to 6,000,000. It is quite impossible to make any more accurate estimate. Even if the lower figure were taken, it would be appalling. One can make a comparison with the

Hitler's triumphant entry into Memel (March 1939), handed over by Lithuania. Hitler is acclaimed as he enters the *Theaterplatz* (Theatre Square).

Pro-German demonstration at Danzig.

losses suffered by the German civilian population in Eastern Europe at the end of the War and under the Russian occupation – estimated at 2,500,000.

The concentration camps had a large number of victims, not merely among the interned Jews, who were not in the majority, but also among the gypsies and other Eastern European populations, consisting of men of the resistance, anti-Nazi politicians and common-law criminals, with whom the Jews were mingled. These people were not solely the victims of execution; they also perished through malnutrition and disease. The famished Germany of the final years of the War obviously took no particular trouble to keep in good health the detainees in its camps.

Millions of men, old and young, women and children, were despatched to the camps to learn their fate, which was at all times

Heydrich and the commander of an *Einsatzgruppe* (Task Force), during the invasion of Poland, September 1939.

terrible, even if not fatal. This must never be forgotten. To these we must add the victims of the four special S.D. groups (the *Einsatzgruppen*), of the Kaminsky Brigade and of the Sonderkommando Dirlewanger in Poland, in the U.S.S.R. and in Yugoslavia, which were responsible for the extermination of Soviet political commissars, Jews and gypsies, including children. The 300 men of the *Einsatzgruppen* must have caused the deaths of several hundreds of thousands of people.

In his book, *Les S.S.* (Culture-Art-Loisirs, 1968), the historian, André Brissaud, says: "At the start, it was not the object of the Nazis to exterminate all the Jews in Europe, but merely to drive them out of the living space of the German people (*die Zurückdrängung der Juden aus dem Lebensraum des deutschen Volkes*). In all the documents which have been found concerning the 'final solution' of the Jewish problem,

After the entry of the German troops into Poland, the members of the German minorities, who had been persecuted since 1919, denounced the authors of their ill-treatment, who were then promptly executed by *Einsatzkommandos* (Commandos) of the S.D.

The Dirlewanger Brigade in action. This unit was set up in 1940 and commanded by an adventurer who had joined the Nazis, Oskar Dirlewanger. He was a former member of a volunteer corps, who later joined the Foreign Legion, became a volunteer in the Condor Legion in Spain, and then set up a *Sonderkommando* responsible for operations against the partisans in Eastern Europe from 1942 onwards. The Brigade was made up of criminal elements who had been recruited in the concentration camps, and it was guilty of appalling atrocities. Dirlewanger was to disappear in 1945, and all the members of his Brigade were executed by the Russians.

the Germans used words having much the same meaning, such as *Ausrottung* (uprooting, elimination) and *Ausschaltung* (exclusion, isolation). Himmler, himself, used expressions such as *Judenevakuierung* (evacuation of the Jews) and *Ausrottung des jüdischen Volkes* (uprooting of the Jewish people) in the particularly virulent speech which he delivered on 4th October 1943 at Poznan. One may well say that the Nazis were camouflaging their true intentions of extermination by the use of anodyne expressions. This is probably true. But the history of anti-semitism under the Third Reich shows that, if the will to systematically exterminate the Jews ever existed, then it was only from the winter of 1941/1942 onwards. The Eichmann trial at Jerusalem, despite its excesses and the passions it aroused, has amply proved this."

For a long time, Hitler and Rosenberg were in favour of dispatching all the Jews to Palestine. Their aim was not to kill them, but to get rid of them from German territory. The State of Israel did not yet exist, and the British were against setting it up at all; because of this, they opposed by all possible means the project of Jewish emigration. Dr. Schacht made an effort in December 1938 to get the British Government to permit the Jews of Austria and Germany to go to Palestine, but he was unsuccessful. In addition, the Jews in question were not at all anxious to go to the Promised Land. *Untersturmführer* (Second Lieutenant) S.S., Leopold von Mildenstein who, even before the War, had been made responsible by Hitler and Himmler to prepare their "return" for them, ended by finding no support.

The Russian engineer, Bronislav Kaminsky, a ferocious anti-Communist, went over to the Germans in 1941, setting up a sort of private militia of about twenty thousand men. These led the hard life of the partisans and used the same methods of terrorism. The formation was called R.O.N.A. (*Russkya Osvoboditelnaya Narodnya Armiya*), the Russian National Free Army. This was administratively incorporated with the Waffen S.S. in March 1944, but it never wore the runes. Its cruelty at the time of the crushing of the revolt at Warsaw resulted in Kaminsky being sent for court martial and executed. His men were assigned to the 38th Division of the Waffen S.S.

Obersturmbannführer (Lieutenant-Colonel) Adolf Eichmann, head of the Sub-department IV B 4 of the R.S.H.A. He obtained the collaboration of a number of Zionist organisations.

"At the time when Eichmann took over the Sub-department IV B 4 in the R.S.H.A., which had been established to settle the Jewish question, he was not himself anti-semitic. His functions led him to collaborate closely with the World Zionist Organisation and to make contact with the leaders of the secret Zionist organisation, *Haganah*. He even went himself to Palestine in 1937, in the company of *Oberscharführer S.S.* (Sergeant-Major) Herbert Hagen, the successor to Leopold von Mildenstein, to examine the problem. When he returned, Eichmann set up office in Vienna. His job was to accelerate Jewish emigration by all possible means, even if this had to be 'forced'. The sub-department IV B 4 of the R.S.H.A. became the central office for Jewish emigration."

By the end of 1939, 150,000 Austrian Jews had left, by choice, to go to live in Palestine, as had also 120,000 German Jews and 78,000 from Bohemia/Moravia. This emigration had been organised by the S.D., with *Haganah*'s approval, and was carried out clandestinely by boat, despite the draconian measures taken by Britain to stop it. The War put a brutal end to this strange alliance in September 1939.

Himmler then ordered Eichmann to find a substitute solution. Faithful to his "Zionism", Eichmann persisted in thinking that it was necessary to provide a national home for the Jews and that this would solve the problem. Following through this conviction, he organised, with Heydrich's approval, a Jewish reserve in Poland, to the south-west of Lublin, near the little town of Nisko. In a few months, 300 000 Jews were directed towards this territory. But the Governor-General of

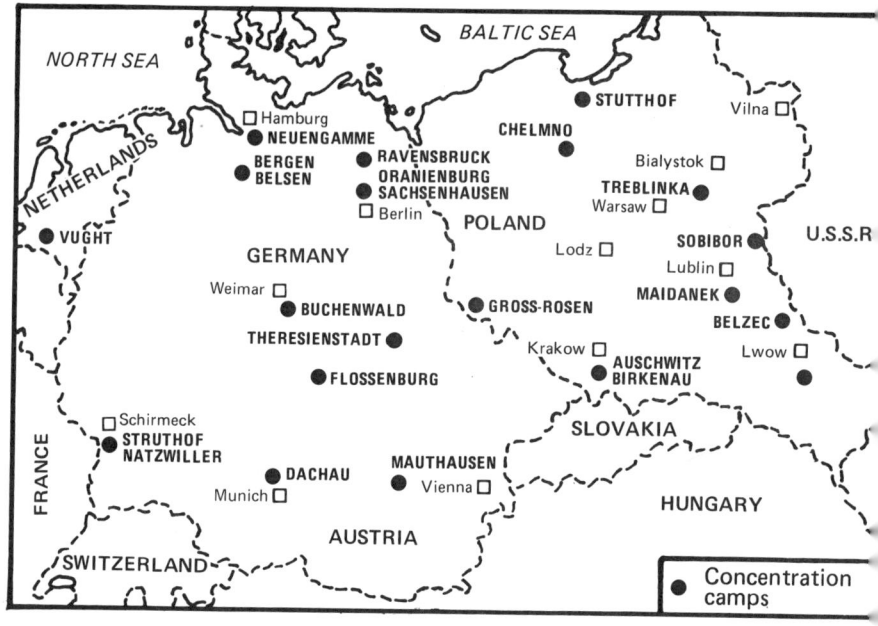

The main concentration camps (Tallandier document).

Poland, Hans Frank, was not at all keen on this solution. He went to Berlin and complained to Goering. He obtained permission to stop the transportations on 13th April 1940. Then Eichmann had another idea – the famous Madagascar Plan. The idea was that France would hand over the island to Germany and that a national Hebrew state would be set up there, capable of taking four million Jews. Himmler and Heydrich approved, and on 18th June 1940 Hitler himself told Mussolini that "an Israeli state might be set up in Madagascar". The project came to nothing.

The attack on the U.S.S.R. in June 1941 upset the German anti-semitic policy. For Hitler, Communist Russia represented the very heart of Jewish subversion. It was in Russia that the Communists had first gained power in 1917, and it was from there that all the revolutionary attempts aimed at Germany and Europe had come since that time. He gave orders for special units to be set up in secret, the *Einsatzgruppen* (Task Forces) of the S.D., whose terms of reference were to effect a physical liquidation of the Communist leaders, readily identified with Russian Jews, as the Wehrmacht advanced over Soviet territory.

A caricature from the Daily Mirror.

The idea of physically exterminating all the Jews of Europe was examined in detail at the Nuremberg Trials.

When Goering was being tried, a directive he had sent to Heydrich on 31st July 1941 was produced. In this he wrote: "I give you all powers to make preparations for ... a final solution to the Jewish question in those of the European territories which are under German influence. ..." Goering was able to show quite easily that "final solution" did not necessarily signify destruction or extermination.

The other trials, particularly the one concerned with the Wilhelmstrasse and the one in respect of the Nazi organisations (S.S., S.D., Gestapo, etc.), threw light on other documents, particularly the Minutes of the Wannsee Conference of 20th January 1942. André Brissaud observes that "the translations of this strange document were as fanciful in French as in English or in Russian." The phrase *die Zurückdrängung der Juden aus dem Lebensraum des deutschen Volkes* (the forcible removal of the Jews from the living space of the German people) was translated into French as "the extermination of the Jews in the living space of the German people".

In point of fact, there is in existence no single German document proving that "the final solution of the Jewish problem" meant "the total liquidation of the Jews". This is not to deny that extermination measures against the Jews were carried out. It is, however, still important to try to arrive at the precise historical truth of whether, apart from the cases of the *Einsatzgruppen*, the S.S. ever received orders to carry out systematically the extermination of the Jews. It is impossible to answer objectively. It is established that the systematic extermination of European Jews actually took place in the "death camps" of Chelmo, Belzec, Sobidor, Maidanek, Treblinka, Auschwitz and others only from the end of 1942 onwards and that it became general during the years 1943, 1944 and, especially, 1945. There were very large numbers of innocent victims.

It would seem that there was a number of different tendencies at work in the various German services, including the S.S. in respect of the Jews. The hawkish tendency was to ignore any distinction and see physical extermination as the only solution. The "doves" on the other hand, remained faithful to the policy of peaceful evacuation which had been in force up to 1941. The difficulty with this second policy was how to keep it going during wartime. The third tendency, finally, was represented by *Obergruppenführer* (Lieutenant-General) Oswald Pohl, the head of the W.V.H.A., who was responsible for the administration of the concentration camps and, thus, for their economic production. For him, the detainees represented above all a source of man-power, and he did all he could to preserve it against the repressive policies of the R.S.H.A.

S.S. *Brigadeführer* (Brigadier) Erich Naumann, former member of the S.A., who joined the S.D. in 1935. He was Commander of *Einsatzgruppe* (Task Force) B in the East from November 1941 to February 1943. At his trial, he referred to Hitler's executive order, and said: "I thought this decree correct, because it formed part and parcel of our war aims; it was thus necessary". He was hanged on 6th June 1951. The photograph shows him at the time of his arrest.

In a curious passage taken from his deposition during his trial, *Obergruppenführer* (Lieutenant-General) Ohlendorf denied the existence of any general policy of extermination, while still recognising that there had taken place numerous executions of Jews who had been taken to the East by the *Einsatzgruppen* under his orders: "I knew nothing of any plans for the extermination of the Jews," he said, "but I did know the history of Communism and the way in which the Bolsheviks had conducted civil war, wars with Finland and Poland and the occupation of the Baltic countries; there was also the denunciation by Russia of the Geneva Conventions.* For them, just as the enemy class had to be destroyed inside the country, so the enemy nation had to be destroyed abroad. In my opinion, the Reich was in a state of emergency, which called for legitimate means of defence. We had no possibility of properly adjudging the situation."

* In the *Gulag Archipelago*, Alexander Solzhenitzyn estimates that, in the space of 33 years (1920 to 1953), there were between 40 and 50 million detainees in the Soviet concentration camps. In the Ukraine alone, the famines brought on by the agrarian policies and the execution of peasants caused some 3 or 4 million to die in 1932 to 1933.

CHAPTER 5

The Blood Myth

Ideology in the Form of a Religion

On 7th September, 1940, at Metz, Hitler gave a speech to the officers of the *Leibstandarte*. For a year now, the War had consecrated the military valour of the S.S., and the prospects of victory seemed to be bright. "I want to set up an Order which shall express and develop the concept of Nordic blood, so that we can attract to ourselves all the Nordic blood in the world, denying it to our adversaries, so that we can carry out our master policy and struggle against others who possess that blood and the values that it represents. We must attract to ourselves Nordic blood, and others must not possess it. This idea and this aim have been in existence for years and have never been jettisoned."

The central credo of the S.S. ideology was the Blood Myth, which evoked, at one and the same time, racial purity and cosmic combat. This was an idea which was familiar to all Germans as a result of the famous story set out in the *Nibelungenlied*, made fashionable by Wagner, according to which Siegfried kills the dragon and bathes in its blood in order to remain invincible. Not only German antiquity, but the whole of European medievalism, was impregnated with this myth.

When Hitler and Himmler talked about an Order of the Templars, responsible for looking after the Holy Grail, the receptacle of the pure blood, they were appealing to medieval tradition, according to which blood is the symbol of honour and fidelity. It was in this sense that the

The Flag of Blood, the mystical symbol of a new religion.

Blutfahne (Flag of Blood) had been piously preserved ever since the shootings of 9th November 1923 in Munich. Every year, Hitler established a mystical link between this flag and the new standards of the S.S. and the S.A. during a solemn baptismal ceremony. The S.S. used to make their vows in front of the *Blutfahne*. Consecrated by the centuries, this ceremonial harked back to the chivalric initiation ceremony by which the suzerain was linked with his vassal by sword, fire and blood. For the S.S., their Führer was like the seigneur, incarnating the eternal principles of life rooted in the ancestral and sacred earth to which the dead would return in order to water and fertilise it with their blood so generously shed.

This mythical value of blood is found constantly throughout all the Orders of chivalry. It was shed blood which united the Knights with each other. Among these Orders, that of the Teutonic Knights was to exercise a particular fascination over the S.S.

Hermann von Salza, founder of the Order of Teutonic Knights and Grand Master from 1210 to 1239. A Waffen S.S. regiment was to bear his name.

Albert of Brandenburg, Grand Master of the Order of Teutonic Knights from 1511 to 1525. He secularised the Order and his Knights married and founded hereditary fiefs in the Baltic countries.

It was no chance that the S.S. colours, black and white, were those formerly worn by the *Deutsche Ritterorden* (Order of Teutonic Knights), which handed them down to Prussia.

The Order was founded in 1198 with the object of aiding German knights who had been wounded or had fallen sick during the Crusades. These soldier monks were distinguished right from the start from the other Orders of hospitallers, the Knights of St. John or the Templars. Their recruitment was exclusively Germanic, and it was this ethnic selection which determined the course taken by the Order. In 1211, the Teutonic Knights abandoned Palestine. The Golden Bull of Rimini entrusted to them the colonisation of the Slavonic lands to the east of the Elbe, with the double patronage of the Pope and Emperor. Inspired by the *Realpolitik* of the Grand Master, Hermann von Salza, the Cross served as a pretext for Germanic expansion.

Ever since antiquity, the lands fringing the Baltic Sea have attracted conquerors. The ancient amber route had seen occur the multiple rising and ebbing of the tides of invasion. Europe met Asia there; there the German confronted the Slav. In these lands of dunes, marshes and forests, the Teutonic Knights were preceded by the Brethren of the Sword, who owed their name to the huge blood-red cross, extended by the shape of a sword, which decorated their white mantles. They founded the city of Riga, crushed the Livonians in 1207 and the Latvians five years later. They pushed back a Danish invasion in 1220, but were defeated in 1229 by a Lithuanian army which was much more powerful. After this disaster, the Brethren joined the Teutonic Knights, to whom they passed on their brief and brilliant tradition.

Dominique Venner has written in her book *Baltikum*: "They handled the plough and the trowel quite as well as the lance and the sword; they built towns and fortresses – Kreuzburg, Kronstadt, Vogelsang, Reden, Marienverder, Elbing, Königsberg, Marienburg. Following the sword of the knight-monks, colonists swept in in great numbers. But they were never numerous enough. The Slavs took advantage of the weaknesses of their conquerors, and even made an alliance with the Tartars to get rid of the German barons. Risings and suppressions succeeded one another, but the Teutonic Order extended its inexorable domination over Prussia and Kurland."

The Order was to reach its height in the second half of the fourteenth century, but it was brought to a remarkable stop in 1410. On 15th July of that year, the Knights were crushed at Tannenberg by a coalition of Poles, Lithuanians and Mongols. The power of the Order was broken, but the memory of its valorous deeds never ceased to haunt German dreams.

Five centuries later, on 30th August 1914, on that same field of battle of Tannenberg, the future Marshal von Hindenburg was to

The castle of Marienburg, in East Prussia, the headquarters of the Grand Master of the Teutonic Order and the sanctuary of the conquering Knights.

An S.S. man keeps vigil in the crypt of the castle of Quedlinburg, where rest the remains of King Henry the First, the Fowler (876 to 936), who fought against the Slavs.

destroy the Slav divisions of General Samsonov. The Germans had forgotten nothing.

The S.S. adopted the myth of the Teutonic Knights for its own purposes, just as it was also inspired by the example set by the Duke of Saxony, Henry the First, the Fowler (876 to 936), elected King of Germany in 919. This clever and patient prince, a member of the German branch of the French Capetian dynasty, imposed his authority over the Grand Duchies, particularly those of Swabia and Bavaria, conquering also Lorraine. He forbade the Church to interfere in State matters. With him, the German drive towards the East began. He fought against the Bohemians and the Slavs to the East of the Elbe and put a stop to Hungarian incursions at the battle of Riade.

Himmler celebrated the memory of Henry the First every year during charismatic ceremonies held in the crypt of the castle of Quedlinburg, where the King had been buried. The first of these commemorative vigils was organised to celebrate the millenary of the death of Henry the First and was held on 2nd July 1936 in the presence of notable guests and the highest dignitaries of the Black Order. In front of the tomb, guarded by armed S.S. men, and in the light of torches, Himmler took the vow to remain faithful to the lessons of the King who had unified the Germans. Following the example of the Grand Master of the Teutonic Order in building his headquarters at Marienburg, Himmler set up at Wewelsburg the command post of the Black Order.

He discovered one day, in a picturesque part of the countryside of Western Germany near Padenborn, in Westphalia, the ruins of a castle dating from the time of the Huns. It was named Wewelsburg – after the Knight Wewel von Büren – and it had been converted in the 17th century. Himmler undertook in 1934 to reconstruct the castle and to make of it the spiritual seminary of his Order. The doors and windows were decorated with blue granite. The grand staircase was protected by a banister of forged iron, decorated with runic motifs. The walls were hung with huge tapestries, depicting Germanic and rural scenes. The woodwork and shelves of the library were of massive oak. Artists presented the Reichsführer S.S. with marble statues of artisans of the ancient Germanic period of grandeur, Henry the First, the Fowler, Henry the Lion, Albrecht the Bear, Frederick Barbarossa, Frederick the Second of Hohenstaufen, and so on (see Andre Brissaud, "Hitler and the Black Order").

The castle of Wewelsburg, the sanctuary of the Black Order.

Plated gorget of the S.S. flagbearers. Regulation 1938 model.

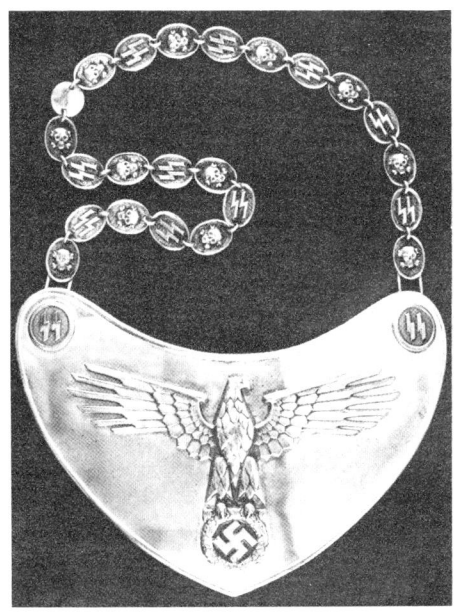

This black and white castle is in the same colours as the S.S. Its massive and impenetrable appearance was the very image of the secrecy with which the S.S. surrounded itself. Wewelsburg was the natural sanctuary of the Nordic élite.

Himmler was inspired by the traditions of the court of King Arthur and set up in Wewelsburg a new community, in the spirit of the old medieval Orders. He formed the habit of receiving twelve heads of the S.S., the most meritorious among them, seated at a round table. While a fire crackled in the monumental chimney, the Black Knights sat down with the *Reichsführer* in huge high-backed leather armchairs around a heavy oak table. Beside each of them was a silver plate engraved with his name on the gilded wood. At night, they went to their rooms, each of which bore the name of a famous figure of the medieval Kingdom and was furnished in medieval style.

Wewelsburg was the spiritual retreat, where the leaders of the S.S. went to meditate, far from the noise of the world outside. Sometimes, in silence, the Black Knights followed the *Reichsführer* into the sanctum of the Order. They had to go down marble steps towards an underground room with ogive arches. The stone walls gave off an impressive chill. In the middle of the room, on a sort of black marble altar, shone out the two white runes of the S.S. At the foot of the altar was another staircase with granite slabs, down which the initiated slowly descended. The *Reichsführer* lit resin torches, one by one. Then a crypt appeared with, at the bottom, a sort of silver cast structure. There, the coats of arms of the leaders of the Black Order were to be incinerated; the bodies would lie above, in the ogive chamber.

All this symbolism, designed with meticulous care by Himmler himself, was aimed at making of the S.S. man a different creature – at forging a spiritual universe, which was at one and the same time both new and rooted in the most ancient German past.

The swearing of the S.S. oath was also marked by chivalric memories. It took place on 20th April, the Fuhrer's birthday, or else on 9th November. Until the beginning of the War, the oath was taken before the Flag of Blood and the black flag marked with S.S. runes.

Two S.S. officers, sword in hand, crossed their blades by touching the poles of the two dipped flags. Four probationers detached themselves from the group which was going to take the oath and advanced two by two – at a goose-step in the case of the *Junker S.S.* and the *Waffen S.S.* They froze to attention, facing each other, on each side of the flags. They placed the middle finger and the forefinger of the left hand on the sword, raised the right hand to the face and took the oath in a loud voice: "I swear to you, Adolf Hitler, Führer of the German Reich, faithfulness and valour. I swear to you and to the leaders appointed by you obedience to death. So help me God!"

The oath was then taken up by the clear voices of the other probationers. A file-past closed the ceremony, to the sound of the *S.S. Marschieren* and the *Horst Wessel Lied*.

The feasts and ceremonies of the new liturgy had, as their purpose, to bring together in thought the whole of the S.S. in a single community. A new calendar took the place of the Christian calendar, in which the year was marked by the Winter and Summer Solstice Feasts, the Anniversaries of the Reich (30th January and 9th November), the Führer's Birthday (20th April) and the Commemoration of Dead Heroes (26th May). In this calendar, the names of the saints of Hebraic origin were struck out and replaced by Germanic names.

The S.S. took the model of chivalry for bringing back the practice of duelling. On 9th December 1935, Himmler decided: "Every S.S. man has the right and duty to defend his honour by arms." With prior consent given by the Reichsführer S.S., every member of the Black

Oath taken by the new recruits to the *S.S. Leibstandarte Adolf Hitler*, 20th April 1936, to celebrate the Führer's birthday.

Order was authorised to demand satisfaction, on condition that his opponent was also a member of the S.S. A number of members of the Order did use this right.

On the day when the oath was taken, every S.S. man received a dagger, the design of which was taken from a Swiss model of the 16th century. On the blade was engraved the S.S. motto: *Meine Ehre heisst Treue* (My honour is loyalty). There was a dagger of honour, which had engraved on it a dedication by the *Reichsführer S.S.*, awarded by Himmler himself for exceptional services. At the end of the War, 362 *Standartenführer* (Colonels) out of 621, 91 *Obergruppenführer* (Lieutenant-Generals) out of 92 and all 4 *Oberstgruppenführer* (Colonel-Generals) in service possessed this dagger.

These myths, these rites and symbols, as we have already said, were not artificial creations. They came from legendary traditions deeply seated in the German popular and intellectual heritage. Richard Wagner had made a powerful contribution in resuscitating them. A wave of intellectual interest in folklore had already, in the 19th century, prepared the way for the appearance of the National Socialist ideology and ritual. The S.S. was to push this tendency to its extreme limits.

Matzke, one of the intellectuals who contributed towards the building of this ideology, wrote: "We do not look at the world from the viewpoint of the soul, but we look at the soul from the viewpoint of the world; thus, everything seems to us clearer, more natural, more apparent."

The historian, André Brissaud, that critical observer of the S.S. phenomenon, has written thus: "It cannot be denied that the Nazis, and especially the S.S. leaders who most completely incarnated the 20th century myth, fell voluntarily into cold-blooded barbarism through attempting, deliberately or unconsciously, by superhuman and at times desperate efforts, to supplant Western moral law impregnated with Christianity, and to bring about what they conceived to be the 'transmutation of the millennium'. There was no question at all of any coexistence within one and the same individual of the two starkest manifestations of being – which we usually call good and evil, spirit and matter, God and the Devil. The S.S. man represented a fusion of all these elements – despite all his multiple and even contradictory aspects – an integrated personality, unified by his existence, his spirit, his

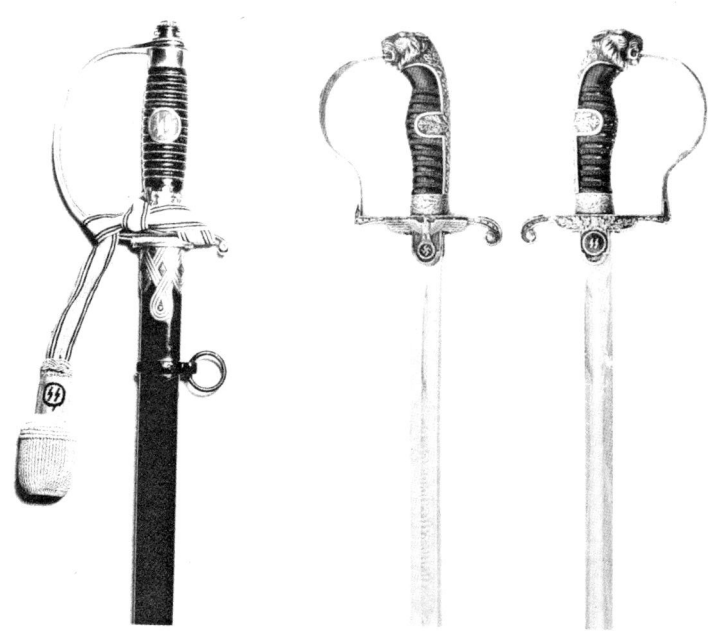

S.S. Officer's sword.   S.S. Officers' sabres.

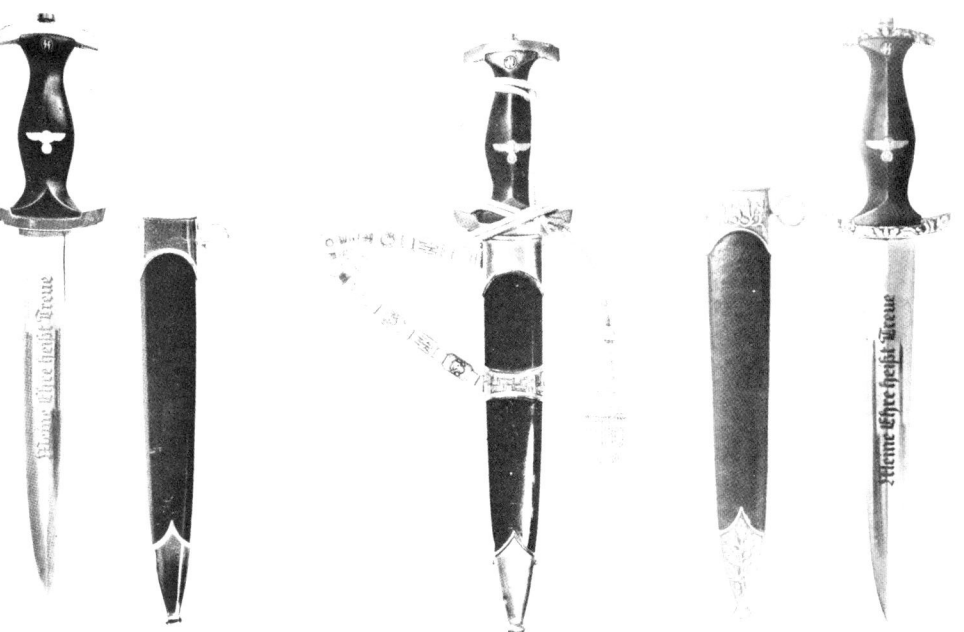

From left to right: regulation S.S. dagger, 1933 model. S.S. officer's dagger, 1936 model. Dagger of honour, awarded for merit.

evolution and his exaggerated metaphysical set-up." We can thus better distinguish the S.S. ideology from the "authoritarian" ideologies of the 20th century, particularly Fascism. It was one of the most pitiless but also one of the most brilliant young leaders of the S.S., *Brigadeführer* (Brigadier) of the S.D., Otto Ohlendorf, who put these differences in a most forcible manner. When he was undergoing trial at Nuremberg (25th July 1947 – 9th April 1948) and was called upon to answer for the extermination which had been perpetrated in the East by the *Einsatzgruppen* under his orders, he gave the following detailed explanation. After retracing his childhood and his joining the National Socialist movement at the age of 18, in 1925, he said:

"I obtained my State doctorate in 1931 and then went for a year to Italy in order to study the manifestations of a political movement which had been already in power for ten years and which was, apparently, parallel to ours. However, I became an anti-Fascist while I was in Italy, and I came back resolved to fight Fascism in all its forms and to keep National Socialism as something different. The dangers of Fascism consisted, for me, of the secularisation of the religious values of Christianity, leading to the dissolution of the community and to the development of individualism and of society's material values. Man no longer belonged to an actual community, and the disappearance of these mystic links has raised questions which have not yet been answered,

S.S. *Brigadeführer* (Brigadier) Otto Ohlendorf: "I became an anti-Fascist when I saw Mussolini's Italy."

whilst at the same time endangering the security of even the greatest countries.

"Fascism developed a humanism which made possible the further elevation of the notion of the State, an absolute State, the basically moral principles of which were nothing but camouflage. National Socialism was diametrically opposed to the ideal of the Fascist State. While admitting that the natural community had been destroyed by individualism, National Socialism tried to consider human beings as realities, having their own values. As members of the community of the people, men saw the development of a relationship to the people as a whole among whom they had been born, realising that they were not members of that community by chance. ..."

"The tragedy of the last War," Ohlendorf went on, "lies in the conflict between two philosophies which have never been properly understood. The purpose of the democratic State is the equality of all citizens and the guarantees of their liberty. But the human side of life (culture, economics and education) is left to the individual, so that there is a dichotomy between the citizen and the human being. It is in this way that this philosophy is opposed to the Germanic tradition."

The S.S. claimed to incarnate this Germanic tradition. Following the racist theoreticians, Himmler meant to preserve it and revivify it above all by the maintenance and selection of hereditary characteristics – hence the importance to the S.S. of all its racial policies.

In January 1937, the *Reichsführer S.S.* delivered a speech concerning the main sectors of the S.S.'s activities, in the course of which he said: "We have a racial department, the positive function of

The Odal rune. Insignia worn on the arm by members of the *Rusha*.

which is ideological education, whilst the security department, on the other hand, has the negative function of rooting out the enemy. The racial department has for the last four or five years been particularly concerned with applications for marriage. No S.S. man may marry

The *Ahnenpass* (the Book of Ancestors), which contained the family tree of each S.S. man, going back in principle to 1750. The cover was printed with the *Rusha* emblem.

without the approval of the *Reichsführer S.S.* We require a medical examination of the fiancée and ideological and human guarantees. In addition, we require to see the list of ancestors going back to 1750, the health certificate of the parents and sundry police information. This takes up a great deal of our time, because many marriages take place. We like our men to be married by the age of 26 and have many children. In addition, this department is concerned with settling the S.S. men in the countryside and with the whole of the ideological education system."

This racial department was called *Rusha* (Rasse und Siedlungshauptamt – Service of Race and Settlement). It was founded in 1931 by Dr. Walter Darré, an agricultural engineer who had been born in the German colony in Argentina in 1895. He was five years older than Himmler, and had done his war service in the Artillery. After the defeat, he decided to become an agriculturist and became interested in stock-rearing problems. He joined the National Socialist Party in 1930, after bringing out his first book *Das Bauerntum als Lebensquelle der nordischen Rasse* (the Peasants as the Vital Source of the Nordic Race).

Darré met Himmler at a meeting of *Artaman* (a movement the aims of which were the settlement of young Germans on their own land). He joined the S.S. and became the first Head of *Rusha*. He summarised all his ideas in a new work, *Neuadel aus Blut und Boden* (New Nobility of Blood and Earth). He became Minister of Agriculture in June 1933 and, the following year, *Reichsbauernführer* (Leader of the Peasants of the Reich).

For Darré, the Germans were both farmers and warriors. Their world was that of both colonisers and heroes, and he recognised no

The headquarters of *Rusha* at Berlin.

Dr. Walter Darré, the founder of *Rusha*, who said: "The disappearance of the peasant is the death of our people."

clear division between the nobility and the peasants. Every free man is noble in essence, since he can bear arms.

Darré noted that Nordism had declined in Germany, and he linked this with the decline among the peasants. He considered that it was necessary to create a new nobility, composed, not of individuals, but of families.

The head of *Rusha* thus intimately linked the concepts of blood and earth. For him, there was no racism without roots. The earth is not made solely to feed people, but also to provide them with physical and moral health. Darré summed up his ideas in a formula: "The death of the peasant is the death of our people. It is not merely bread which grows in furrows; it is men also." Darré considered Christianity to be an evil influence, destroying the original concept of Germanism.

An ideological quarrel brought Darré into conflict with Himmler in 1936. At that time, the *Reichsführer S.S.* was thinking about colonising the east of Europe, as a solution to German problems. This expansionist vision was opposed by Darré, who considered that the destiny of the German man was to be brought up within his own frontiers and not to conquer new lands. This difference of opinion took an acid turn, and Darré had to give up his leadership of *Rusha*. He was replaced by Otto Hofmann, then, later, by *S.S. Obergruppenführer* (Lieutenant-General) Richard Hildebrandt. He died in 1953, after serving a term of imprisonment after the War.

Responsible, as it was, for watching over the racial regeneration of the German people and the selection of its élite *Rusha* intervened during the War, in Poland and in the territories of the East, to promote there the settlement of German colonists. It thus established the conditions under which the indigenous populations could either be assimilated or be rejected by German ethnics.

Another of *Rusha*'s functions was to maintain at all times selectivity within the body of the S.S. itself, at first in a rough fashion and then, later, on ever more exact principles. In Himmler's view, only those who were racially pure could be considered Germans.

This selection was not limited to men, for its purpose was to preserve pure parentage. For this reason, every member of the S.S. was required to marry a woman of similar quality. From one year to the next, the severity of the measures designed to preserve the purity of the S.S. was increased.

In this sphere, *Rusha* played the role of a marriage counsellor. It guided the choice of S.S. applicants for marriage and encouraged large families. Thanks to its influence, S.S. men who were suitable for colonisation were able to obtain a personal estate in the east.

The principles and the organisation of the S.S. concerning

"Preserving men of good blood."

engagement and marriage were laid down in an order from Himmler on 31st December 1931, more than a year before taking over power:

1) *The S.S. is an association of German men, defined according to their Nordic blood and specially selected.*

2) *In conformity with the National Socialist conception of the world, and recognising that the future of our people is founded on selection and the preservation of good racial blood, free from all taint of hereditary disease, I am now requiring members of the S.S. to obtain our authorisation before marriage.*

3) *The target we pursue is the protection of our precious German heredity, free from the taint of all hereditary disease and defined in accordance with the qualities of the Nordic man.*

4) *Consent to marry is given or refused only as a function of racial principles and with a view to congenital health.*

5) *Every S.S. man who wishes to marry must obtain the authorisation of the* Reichsführer S.S.

6) *Members of the S.S. who marry in spite of being refused an authorisation will be dismissed from the S.S.*

7) *The practical work in connection with marriage authorisations will fall upon the Service of Race and Population* Rusha *of the S.S.*

"To become mothers of the children of soldiers."

On 28th November 1939, that is, shortly after the opening of the War, Hitler signed a new order for the S.S.:

Order to all the S.S. and the Police.

Every war involves a shedding of the best blood. A multitude of victories means a loss of vigour and blood. The death of the best is not the worst fate. What is worse is the absence of children who have not been procreated by the living during the war and cannot be procreated after the war.

Quite apart from the civil laws and normal customs, it must now be the duty of all German women and girls of good blood to become mothers of the children of soldiers going to the Front, not frivolously, but seriously.

The future of these children will be ensured as follows:

1) *Official guardians will take over the wardship, in the name of the* Reichsführer S.S., *of all legitimate or illegitimate children of good blood whose fathers have fallen in the War.*

2) *The S.S. will look after legitimate and illegitimate children procreated during the War.*

3) *The* Rusha *will keep the* Sippenbuch S.S. *(S.S. Parentage Book).*

4) *The* Reichsführer S.S., *the Director of* Rusha *and the experts of that Service, bind themselves on their honour to observe discretion.*

5) *S.S. men must clearly see that, with this Order, they have performed an act of great importance. Mockery, disdain and non-comprehension will not affect us; the future is ours.*

Gundrund, Himmler's daughter, in 1935.

"The *Lebensborn* (Fount of Life) will house and look after the future mothers of good racial value, having a good biological heredity." *Himmler.*

It was no doubt an audacious stroke at such a time to ensure official aid to mothers who were not married and to children who were illegitimate. It is, further, quite within National Socialist ideology to make plain that destiny affected by arms is not in itself decisive and that the most important thing remains the preservation and the transmission of German biological "capital". The mission of the S.S. was, therefore, not only to eliminate the foes of the Third Reich, but also to bring to birth a new generation of children of good race. Births had to be promoted without taking into account whether the parents were married or not, and it was also necessary to bring up the children born from these unions.

This was the role of the *Lebensborn* (Fount of Life), founded in 1936 and, as was the case with the *Ahnenerbe* (Heritage of the Ancestors), it was attached to Himmler's personal Staff. The aim was clearly defined in an Order of the Day on 13th September 1936:

Himmler had been very impressed by the Finnish organisation of the *Lottas-Svard*, created by Mrs. Fanny Luukkonen to "discharge the Finnish militia and soldiers from all the tasks that were not directly concerned with combat." He later set up the *S.S. Hilferinnen* (S.S. Auxiliary force). The women in this force were measured by the same racial criteria as the men, and the S.S. were called upon to regard them as equals and comrades.

"Four children are the minimum for a good and healthy marriage. If there are no children in a household, every Führer S.S. must adopt children of good racial value, free from the taint of hereditary disease, raise them in Nazi doctrine and give them training suitable to their aptitudes.

The *Lebensborn* association is available to Führer S.S. for the purpose of:

1) *Sustaining the families with many children of good racial value, having a good biological heredity.*

2) *Finding a home for and looking after the future mothers of good racial value and having a good biological heredity, a careful examination of whom had indicated the probability that they would have children of the same value.*

3) *Looking after the children.*

4) *Looking after the mothers of the children.*

Himmler added the words: "I shall personally look into the success of my Order."

Much has been written, and a number of extremely frank films have also been shown, indicating that *Lebensborn* was nothing but a "human stud farm". Details have even been given about the organisation of meetings for reproductive purposes between girls and selected young men. Nothing is lacking in such rendezvous; not even the moonlight is missing from these hurried idylls. The fact is, there were eight confinement houses and six children's homes. The organisation was to develop as the War went on. Thus, foreign children, orphans, or even children who had been torn from their Polish, Czech or Serbian families because they were recognised as being of Nordic race and should, therefore, be raised according to National Socialist principles – like the Janissaries of the Ottoman Empire – were accepted into *Lebensborn* homes. Eighty thousand children were thus "Germanised" by *Lebensborn*.

It was the same concern to ensure the future of the race which was behind Himmler's Special Order of 15th August 1942. This indicated that, when an S.S. family had only one son left and he was of military age, he would be withdrawn from the Front and sent home for a year in order to have children and preserve his lineage. The young man concerned received an order in these terms:

1) *On the Führer's orders, you have been withdrawn from the Front because you are the last son of your family. This measure is being taken*

because the people and the State are interested to ensure that such families as yours do not die out.

2) *It has never been the custom of the S.S. blindly to accept what Fate decrees without doing anything to change it. It is your duty to have children of good blood as quickly as possible, so that you will no longer be the "last son".*

3) *Aim to guarantee the survival of your ancestors and families in the course of the next year, so that you will be able to return to the fight.*

The *Reichsführer* did not limit his concern to the children of the S.S. All little Europeans, promoted to the dignity of blood brothers (this notion was to be greatly enlarged), were assured of vigilant attention, not without quite a few afterthoughts, as will be seen. This attitude presents a violent contrast to the indifference manifested towards the suffering of Jewish children, for example. On 20th May 1944, Himmler sent a letter, marked "Secret", to *Obergruppenführer* (Lieutenant-General) Artur Phelps, commander of the Fifth Mountain Corps of the S.S. in the Balkans:

"Dear Phelps, I consider it very important that children without parents from all the Balkan regions be brought together by our divisional commanders. This measure is necessary for the following reasons:

Insignia of the *S.S.*
Hilferinnen (S.S. Auxiliaries
– the Women's Force).

1) We are Germans, and we cannot see unmoved the innocent children of a worthy and brave people being side-tracked and lost as a result of unfortunate circumstances.

2) If they do survive, such young people will follow one of two currents of thought; either they will go over to Communism, if we do nothing for them, or they will come to us if we do.

I have set aside places in school for these poor orphans, and I shall set up special establishments so that the Croat State will find in them worthy men and valuable citizens, once order and security have returned. Please order the commanders of divisions under your orders to group together all young orphans of both sexes. I expect to be informed every month of the number of children so gathered together by each division. I would request you to ensure that these children are transported to the Reich from the places where they are grouped together, in collaboration with *S.S. Obergruppenführer* (Lieutenant-General) Berger, to whom I have issued orders to make places available in schools and homes which he will also organise."

"These are our daughters and sisters, who are destined to be the fiancées and wives of our S.S. men. Later when a man is to marry a girl and when he learns that she has been an Auxiliary in the S.S., he will say: 'I can marry her — she will be all right.' That is how it should be." Himmler, 4th October, 1943.

The "Janissaries of the Third Reich".

This letter was confirmed on 14th July 1944 by a note sent to *Obergruppenführer* (Lieutenant-General) Gottlob Berger:
"Dear Berger,
You will have received by now a copy of the letter that I wrote on 20th May 1944 to *S.S. Obergruppenführer* Phelps. I am charging you, as I have already told you verbally, to raise these young orphans like 'Janissaries'. Will you please give your customary energetic attention to this problem, in order to find a solution, so that we can return to the states concerned men who are worthy and citizens of value once order and stability have been restored. At the same time, the Reich will have in these people faithful supporters of the Führer and future soldiers to mount guard, as of old, on the frontiers of the Reich."

In addition to its task of racial defence, *Rusha* was responsible, in collaboration with the *S.S. Hauptamt* (S.S. Central Office), headed by *Obergruppenführer* Gottlob Berger, and with the *Ahnenerbe*, actively to practise neo-pagan rituals, including the "Julfest" (Yule Feast) and S.S. marriages and baptisms.

An S.S. marriage was not celebrated by a priest; the bride and groom exchanged their rings in the presence of the commander of an S.S. unit, who handed to them bread and salt, symbolising life.

The S.S. man must ensure his family's continuance.

To show the interest that the S.S. had in all births, the organisation gave presents to the family. At the birth of their first child, Himmler sent the parents a ribbon and a bib of blue silk. These articles were manufactured in the S.S. workshops at Allach. On the birth of the fourth child, he sent a letter of congratulation and a silver Teutonic candelabrum, bearing the engraved words: "You are but a link in the eternal racial chain."

There was a particularly impressive S.S. baptism on 4th February 1937 at Gmund am Tegernsee, when the first boy (following two girls) was born to Karl Wolf, the head of the *Reichsführer's* Staff. He received the first name of Thorisman on the day before he became one year old. The ceremony took place in the presence of Heinrich Himmler and four godfathers, including Reinhard Heydrich.

Each of the godfathers spoke in turn. The first offered him the blue ribbon of life and said: "May the blue ribbon of loyalty mark all his existence. Whoever is a German and feels he is a German must be loyal. Birth and marriage, life and death, are symbolically united by this blue ribbon. May this child form part of the family and the unit. I wish that he may become a true boy and a complete German man."

The second offered him a cup and said: "The source of all life is God: may your knowledge, your duty, the purpose of your existence and all revelation come from God! May every sip taken from this cup bear witness that you are bound to God."

The third offered him a spoon and said: "May this spoon nourish you until you attain man's estate. May your mother also give witness to you of her love, and may she chastise you by depriving you of food if you transgress the laws of God."

The fourth offered him the family ring, and said: "This ring, the ring of the Wolf family and of the S.S. unit, will be worn by you, my child, when you become a young man and show yourself worthy of the S.S. and your unit."

It was Heinrich Himmler himself who gave the child his first names: "At the desire of your parents, and as instructed by the S.S., I give you the names of Thorisman Heinrich Karl Reinhard. It shall be your responsibility, parents and godparents, to cultivate in this child a true and courageous German heart, following the will of God. To you, my dear child, I wish that you shall show yourself worthy of the proud name of Thorisman, retaining the characteristics it confers after you have attained man's estate and throughout your life. So be it!"

The flames of the bonfire can also fuel the pyres of the Inquisition.

The reader will note the frequent invocation of "God" in the course of this ceremony. Although this God was very different from that of the Christians, the concept was basically the same – the S.S. was not atheist.

On 22nd December 1938, the *Schwarzes Korps* gave some rein to the religious concepts of the S.S. at Christmas time, that is, *Julfest*:

"The religions of the world may well call themselves universal and preach what they call 'the one-ness of the Christian people', but the peoples of foreign blood have never properly understood the profound symbolism of Christmas.

The Magi of the East today cast frightened glances in the direction of the bright flame that we are lighting in the nights of the Winter Solstice. This flame is not for us the flame of sacrifice; it is not some old buried custom. This flame is for us the clear sign of life; it is God smiling over the earth, a God who has called his creation to life and not to death.

The flame burns throughout the night. For us, this hour is not one of bewitched obscurity. This flame lighting up the starry vault is for us the symbol of the unity of nature and life. Day and night, body and soul, light and shade, all is comprehended in the eternal cycle of the fertility of Time. Watch over this flame, comrades, for fire, light and sun are the most sacred of our possessions."

CHAPTER 6

The Reichsführer's Cadets

The Napolas – Schools for Future Leaders of the Third Reich

On 20th April 1933, Dr. Bernhard Rust, the Reich Minister of Education, set up schools to train the future Germanic élite. They were given the name of *Napolas* (*Nationalpolitische Erziehungsanstalten* – National Political Institutes of Education). The first of these was at once opened north of Hamburg, against the austere backcloth of the castle at Plön; up to 1918, it had been one of the most famous schools of Prussian cadets. The white silhouette of the castle rises above a romantic landscape of lakes, sandy stretches and forests. Clusters of red standards with swastikas flapped in the northern wind, which also brought at times the echo of rough soldiers' songs.

Like the other *Napolas*, Plön was a closed universe, dedicated to the Führer's vow: "We will cause to grow up a youth before which the whole world will tremble – a youth which is forceful, imperious, intrepid and pitiless. This is what I want. I want in this organisation nothing feeble or tender. I want these young soldiers to have the strength and beauty of young deer."

Everything here was designed to celebrate the body. The *Napola* had a covered riding school with a stable, two halls for sport, playgrounds and a boathouse, but no swimming bath – because the castle is on the side of a lake. There was swimming and sailing. In winter, the water was iced over for a whole month, and skating then went on.

Hitler addresses the future instructors of the first leaders' schools in 1933, at a meeting at Bernau.

The walls of the high rooms and the white corridors were covered with slogans beneath the coloured flags, such as: "Praise that which hardens you" – the first thing that new pupils saw, once they had crossed the threshold, and "Chase not the hero from your heart", an aphorism from Nietzsche. Further along, at the entrance to a classroom: "Write in blood and you will learn that blood is mind." In a dormitory was written: "Love life like a combat and death like an adventure."

Every *Napola* was directed by a *Kommandeur* (Commandant), with an adjutant called *Anstaltsleiter* (*Alei* – Director of the Institute). The pupils, called *Jungmannen* (literally "young men") were split up into *Hundertschaften* (Centuries), each of which was commanded by a *Hundertschaftführer* (Centurion) of their own age, assisted by an adult instructor who was an S.S. officer or non-commissioned officer. Each Century was divided into three *Züge* (Columns), each of which had thirty or so *Jungmannen*, and these made up one class. They were supervised by a *Zugführer*, who was more of a playleader than a form master. Every *Zug* constituted a community, having its own table in the refectory, its own dormitory and its own sporting equipment. Instructors and *Jungmannen* lived together all the time. This community life was fundamental to the pedagogy of the *Napolas*. The classes were identical in scholastic structure to those of the ordinary German schools of the time, ranging from the *Sexta* (First Form) to the *Abitur* or *Reifeprüfung* (G.C.E. Form).

To get into a *Napola*, the candidate had to pass a very difficult

The "Ordensburg" (Castle of the Order) at Sonthofen (*Ullstein*). The *Ordensburgen*, initially called *Führerschulen* (Leaders' Schools) were first set up by the S.A., but they gradually passed into the control of the S.S. There were also *Hitlerschulen* (Hitler Schools), controlled by the Party to train its own cadets. The *S.S. Junkerschulen* (S.S. Junker Schools), training the future officers of the Waffen S.S., and the *Napolas* completed the range of the higher political schools of the Third Reich.

The great conference hall at the Ordensburg of Grossinsee.

The Ordensburg at Vogelsang, set up for higher ideological education.

examination, which was designed to assess his intellectual, moral and physical standard. Only boys who proved to have the highest qualities were accepted.

The curriculum included instruction in National Socialist politics. The study of biology was not limited to the laws of heredity but embraced, among other things, what we would now call ethology, the science of behaviour and knowledge of the environment. Typical themes of study were chlorophyll, the birds and their seasons, the significance of the laws for the protection of the forests, and so on. The role of music was also most important although it was not, properly speaking, a "subject" like mathematics. Nevertheless, it impregnated the whole life of the *Napola*; the boys talked music during the breaks, for example of the concert they had just heard at Marienburg or in the school hall. They sang from morning to evening, from the hoisting of the flag to the last hour of the day, including the marching songs which accompanied all their walks during the day.

Ideology was a feature which was never far from the curriculum, as shown by the following subjects for essays, set at Oranienstein:

"Throughout the study of history, it is not a matter of learning by heart all about historical facts, but of following the current of the unchanging German blood, of German culture and of the history of the German people. ... In the study and appreciation of the works of art of our ancestors, we search for the sources and background of our own manner of living."

The future *Jungmannen* of the *Napolas* were chosen from the Hitler Youth on the basis of their leadership qualities and their intellectual and physical standards. They entered the school at the age of ten and left it at seventeen, having gained their *Abitur* (G.C.E.). They could then enter the University or a special S.S. or Wehrmacht officers' school.

The training of the *Napolas* set great store by sport. Reference was often made to the education of the medieval knights, which was also centred around sport. The Minister of Education, Bernhard Rust, was convinced that this had no harmful effect whatsoever on learning. "The *Napolas* are proof that a complete physical education favours the raising of intellectual levels by stimulating energy and health."

The pupils' daily exercises rapidly led to a sporting specialisation – fencing, horse-riding, boating, sailing, motor-cycling, shooting. There were inter-school competitions every year in sporting events. The pupils camped for the occasion and to get to their camp they used the same forms of transport which figured in their specialised sport. On their way to the camp, they had to note down their topographical and social observations and write up complete reports.

Every summer, the *Napolas* abandoned their castles and left, with rucksacks on their backs, for the roads of Germany towards the canvas forests near the contested regions of the frontiers. They spent the days in sport, parades and marches, and the evenings around camp fires, when the pupils organised festivities, accompanied by songs and recitations. This is what one pupil said about one of these camps, which was near the German region of Memel – it had belonged to Poland since 1919: "We used to march through the woods, jumping over water-filled ditches. There was a tremendous peace throughout the whole countryside. The wind seemed to be whispering to us of past centuries, the wars of the Teutonic Knights against the Lithuanians and the deeds and exploits of our ancestors. It brought to us the murmuring of our comrades under foreign rule the other side of Memel. We came to the mouth of a river, following a narrow path – it flowed gently, making little waves. Was the countryside the same on the other side? Do the people who live there talk the same language as we do? Why is their frontier here? It makes my blood boil when I think about this injustice. Further to the north, at Tilsit, there's a big bridge which joins the two banks – but we can't go across it. Darkness throws a huge veil over the valley. We sit down and think. Voices of the same people as we are are calling to us, even over frontiers that man has made."

A further important aspect of the educational method applied in the *Napolas* was work in the countryside. Every first-former had to do agricultural work for 6 to 8 weeks every year, being lodged and fed in a farmhouse. The aim was to teach the future leaders about the peasants

Sport was an important feature of the education.

A *Wandertag* (a Day in the Country). The boys go for a route march, their rucksacks on their backs, singing. The black flag carries the *Sieg-Rune* (the Victory Rune), common to the S.S. and the *Deutsches Jungvolk* (German Youth).

of their country, so that they would know more of their lives and be later capable of directing them. The *Jungmann* had to merge himself fully into the life of the countryside, and to experience for himself the hardness of the peasants' life. In this way, he was meant to acquire first-hand experience, going far beyond theoretical knowledge, and National Socialism considered this an indispensable acquisition for those who were in future to hold command posts. This work took place in exposed frontier regions and in those which were politically important for the Reich.

This is what a pupil, who had been sent to a farmhouse in the Warthegau, said about his relationship with the peasant in whose house he was lodged: "The peasant is the master of the land. His orders alone are what count. He's awfully dour, and he never laughs. Now I know why. He suffered a lot during the Polish occupation. On 26th August 1939 the Poles came and arrested his son, and he himself was deported, along with the other Germans in the village. All this Polish domination left awful memories with him. You can't talk to him about them any more. All this ill-treatment has made the peasants here hard and mistrustful, but once you've overcome their distrust, they open up and welcome you with open arms. In the evenings, we all sit down at the same table as the peasants, we've all become real pals. They've taught us a lot, and they were very happy that they were able to show us something."

In the same way, the *Jungmannen* in the *Napolas* worked in the mines for eight weeks during their seventh year at school. The purpose of these eight weeks was the same – to teach the future leaders to understand better those people who have to work hard for their living. A further advantage of working in the mine was that it forced the boys both to spend and to economise on the money they earned. What they did not spend went into the *Napola* Fund. This provided a pool with which, for example, the pupils at Oranienstein often invited the families who had put them up to come to see them.

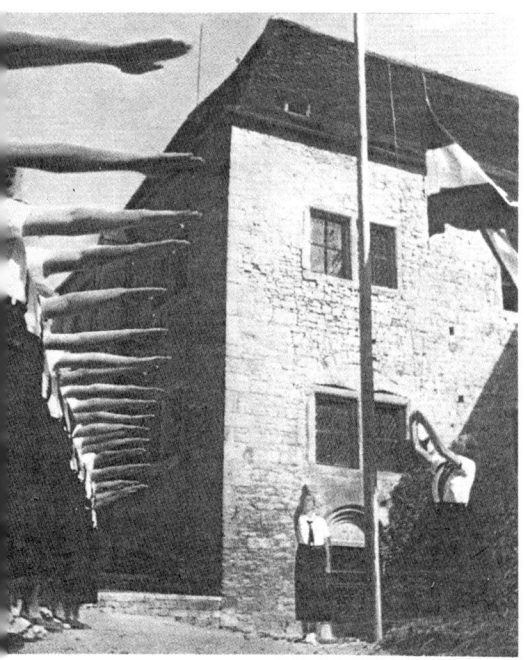

Hoisting the flag at the School of Girl Cadets (Hitler Youth) at Freiburg.

It was also expected of the boys that they would to some extent influence the political opinions of their work-mates.

Bonds of friendship were forged between the future leaders of the Reich and the worker families. One mother wrote to one of the boys who had lived in her house: "Dear Werner, Thank you for your letter. It shows us that you haven't forgotten us. Even though we did have little differences of opinion at times, this shows that we were really still both of the same mind. When you left, with Wolfgang, I wanted to cry. Every time I go and look at the room where you lived, I think of your tired eyes every morning when I woke you at 5 o'clock. On the day you left, I wanted to sing you a farewell song, but my mother's heart was too heavy. I would like us to keep writing. Give Wolfgang my love."

The *Napolas* also organised trips abroad, so that the *Jungmannen* would come into contact with other ideas and other political systems. These visits were organised to Britain, Africa, the U.S.A. and Mexico. With Britain, there were even some exchanges between schools, but the *Jungmannen* often had to contend with much political hostility. One of them wrote: "I've just spent a weekend with my English penfriend. I felt I had to talk quite a lot about the Führer and Germany, because I saw how much wrong information the English had got about us; they were even angry about us. Everywhere I went, I came up against untruths, which I felt I had to oppose. Time was short, but I really think I did convince the English that we meant well."

During the War, the bombing made it necessary to evacuate children from the towns, and this was organised by the Hitler Youth. From 1942 onwards the pupils of the upper forms of the *Napolas* were

Jungmannen became both teachers of children and future soldiers.

The *Reichsführer S.S.* inspects his cadets. Among the persons standing in the foreground we can see a Napola instructor in uniform.

regarded as particularly suitable for organising the camps where these pupils stayed, and this service took the place at times of work in the fields and mines. The *Jungmannen* imposed a thoroughly martial discipline on these camps. One of the children on whom this responsibility was conferred wrote: "We used to sound reveille at 6.30. An hour and a half later, we were ready for breakfast. All the rooms had to be spotless, the beds had to be made and squared off, the chairs had to be shone and the dust had to be removed. After the ceremony of hoisting the flag and after the orders for the day had been given, there was school until midday. After a short break, following the midday meal, activities began: either we had sport, or we did manual work or organised our own games. In the evenings there was recreation with songs and talks. Bedtime was at 9.30. Towards the end of my stay in the camp, a trip was organised with the small boys, and they were able to inspect tanks and armoured vehicles – which they did with great enthusiasm. Some of the boys had the luck to have a ride on a tank ..."

Another type of service transformed the *Jungmannen* into anti-aircraft auxiliaries. The Army noted, from the start of the War, that the *Napola* boys made remarkable officers. Thus, the various Army organisations made great efforts to recruit boys from the *Napolas*, and the Army Staffs arranged that military studies took a larger place in the curriculum. Goering arranged, for the Luftwaffe, that special training was given to future pilots, and *Napolas* in the proximity of the sea were deluged by advice from the Navy. The Wehrmacht, for its part, organised courses at its instruction centres.

Special efforts in this direction were made by the Waffen S.S., who considered the *Napolas* as a privileged nursery. One *Jungmann* from a *Napola* in Bohemia/Moravia was invited by the Waffen S.S. to take part in an outing, and this is how he described his first contact with the S.S.: "We arrived at Prague station, and some non-commissioned officers were waiting for us. We looked with admiration at their decorations. They then took us to our quarters — 150 pupils from all the *Napolas* in the Reich. The next day, we looked round the sights of Prague, which clearly showed that that town is German. In the afternoon, at the University, a doctor in the S.S. talked about his work to us and demonstrated to us the heavy responsibility and the never-ending work of the doctor in the front line. The next day was the most interesting of all to us; we took part in combat exercises against tanks and artillery fire, and we also took part in the training programme

All German youth took part in pre-military training.

for sharp-shooters. We're certainly not likely to forget that day!"

The Waffen S.S. was able to be proud of this recruitment programme, for the former *Napola* pupils made excellent officer material. They paid for it very dearly, however. Tributes paid to the *Napolas* call attention to an incredible number of heroic deeds, as described in this letter from a former pupil of the *Napola* at Köslin: "I'm proud to have been a pupil of the *Napolas*. There are a lot of former pupils here in the Waffen S.S., and during the Poland campaign they proved that they were the élite of the élite. In our Company, it was they who fought best. Only two were killed, and three were wounded. One of my comrades had come from the *Napola* at Ilfeld. We had been there for three hours, exposed to constant firing, and he was about ten yards away from me. Like me, he was a machine-gunner. He was just trying to change the position of his gun, when a bullet hit him in the shoulder and another one in the chest. With his last gasp, he called to the sergeant: 'Gunner Number 1 has been killed.' There was no cry of pain. A minute later, he was dead."

The father of a pupil wrote to the *Napola* which his son had attended: "We can still scarcely believe that our dear son will never return. He left us only three months ago, at the end of the holidays. He

When War came, the S.S. instructors gave the *Jungmannen* lessons in battle drill.

Viking and S.S. insignia together.

had already been seriously wounded once, and had lost an eye. In spite of this, he insisted on going back to the front. From being a boy, he had always wanted to follow the Führer. His short faithful life has ended in sacrifice."

The following will was found on a dead boy, dedicated to the *Napola* where he had studied: "I spent three years between your walls – the most beautiful years of my life. You gave a clear form to my idealism. You taught me to believe in the eternal German Reich. You gave sense to my life. You were a second Fatherland for me. None of those who have been brought up by you will ever be able to forget you. You drove each one to an unceasing, obstinate and indefatigable labour for Germany. Never did I forget the words: 'Believe, obey, fight'. From them, I drew inexhaustible resources of energy. As long as you burn these words in the hearts of the young men who are your pupils, you will be and will remain what you should be. If I have no child, please permit me to make over to you the 100 Marks in my pay-book. The best pupils can be given this as a present, in the form of books. In the hope of victory and in the faith of the eternity of the Reich, your former pupil greets you."

The concept of the *Napolas* had come from a War veteran and S.A. leader, Joachim Haupt, in 1933. What he had in mind was something between the former schools of imperial cadets and a British public school.

What was common to the *Napolas* and the British public schools was that the curriculum comprised, not merely intellectual disciplines, but an equal amount of sporting activity. In addition, the *Napolas* allotted much of the time to manual labour, the purpose being to form a young élite, brought up on National Socialist doctrine, with a personal knowledge of practical life as well as theoretical pursuits. However, unlike the public schools, entry into a *Napola* was not dependent on the social and financial position of the parents, but on the personal worth of the future pupil.

The sites chosen for the *Napolas* were outside the large towns and in beautiful natural surroundings. The buildings were those of the former cadet schools, in requisitioned castles or monasteries, and their number went up from year to year. There were 42 of them by the end of 1944, sited throughout the Germanic territories from Alsace to East Prussia.

From the start, they were directed by high grade educationalists, with tried and tested National Socialist principles, chosen rather for their qualities of character than for their university attainments.

All the Reich institutions – S.A., Party or Army – tried to attract the *Jungmannen* and the *Napolas* into their own sphere of influence. For instance, Dr. Robert Ley, head of the Labour Front, tried to do this in the Party's name. When his project encountered opposition from Himmler, he set up the Adolf Hitler Schools in 1937. These did not come under the Ministry of Education, and they were supported by Baldur von Schirach, the leader of the Hitler Youth. However, their importance was considerably less than that of the *Napolas*.

As always, Himmler acted with the utmost skill. From the time of the first public festivities organised by the *Napolas* in 1934, he was always present as an honoured guest. He also appeared at all sporting events. From 1934 onwards, the S.S took responsibility for paying for the equipment and clothing of the *Napolas*. Then, on 9th March 1936,

"My German Youth. You, my young men and girls, must fulfil what we hope for and expect from the Germany to come. If we want a Germany of strength, then you must be strong. If we want a Germany of power, then you must be powerful. If we want once more to form a Germany of honour, then you must have honour yourselves. If we want before us a Germany of order, then you must have order within your ranks. If we once more want to win Germany over to loyalty, then you yourselves must learn to be loyal. You are the Germany of the future, and we want you to be as that Germany of the future should be and must be". *Adolf Hitler.*

Meine deutsche Jugend! Was wir vom kommenden Deutschland ersehnen und erwarten, das müßt ihr, meine Jungens und Mädchen, erfüllen. Wenn wir ein Deutschland der Stärke wünschen, so müßt ihr einst stark sein. Wenn wir ein Deutschland der Kraft wollen, so müßt ihr einst kraftvoll sein. Wenn wir ein Deutschland der Ehre wiedergestalten wollen, so müßt ihr einst Träger dieser Ehre sein. Wenn wir ein Deutschland der Ordnung vor uns sehen wollen, müßt ihr die Träger dieser Ordnung sein. Wenn wir wieder ein Deutschland der Treue gewinnen wollen, müßt ihr selbst lernen, treu zu sein.

Ihr seid das Deutschland der Zukunft und wir wollen daher, daß ihr so seid, wie dieses Deutschland der Zukunft einst sein soll und sein muß. — Adolf Hitler

"It doesn't matter how many glasses of beer a boy can down, but how many blows he can take; it doesn't matter how many nights out he can take, but how many kilometres he can march."
Adolf Hitler.

Himmler was able to arrange for the exclusion of the S.A. man, Joachim Haupt, and for the appointment of S.S. *Obergruppenführer* (Lieutenant-General) Heissmeyer as Inspector General of the *Napolas*. First, the S.S. took control of the schools in Prussia, and then, in 1939, of the schools throughout the Reich. Although, strictly speaking, he came under the Ministry of Education, in fact Heissmeyer received orders from Himmler alone. During the War, he had to oppose attempts made to absorb the Napolas into the Army – the Wehrmacht was proposing that pupils leaving school at 17 should have a rank in the Army and that each school would have a training command, consisting of an officer, a sergeant and six instructors. Himmler was completely opposed to this plan: "There can be no question of reforming the cadet schools on any other than National Socialist principles. I alone am competent to decide on the direction to be taken by the *Napolas*. It is my responsibility to determine their relationship to the Army."

By 1940, the Black Order was able to announce its complete takeover of the *Napolas*, acquiring the powers of decision in matters of selection, curriculum, and teaching staff.

From 19th May 1941 onwards, the selection of the future *Jungmannen*, as indeed that of all members of the S.S., was handed over to *Rusha*. The *Napola* inspectors relied on the S.S. services, particularly the S.D., to find premises in the occupied territories. The commandants and instructors in the *Napolas* were automatically integrated into the S.S. hierarchy and subjected to its discipline. The fight against Christianity became sharper. During the years 1933 to 1936, religion was still an official subject in the curriculum of the *Napolas*. After the subject was abolished in 1936, the boys still had the right to practise a religion, but, as the years went on, this right was more and more contested, until the day when it disappeared completely. A complete break with the Church was then required of all pupils.

The Haselünne affair showed how deep the conflict went. The convent at Haselünne had been requisitioned in 1943, to be turned into a *Napola*. Founded in the Ems region, its history went back to 1652, when it had been put in the hands of the Ursuline Sisters to educate the girls of the neighbourhood. At the start of the War, there were only 200 pupils left. However, the convent still had much influence in the region and the local people were very indignant when they learnt that the S.D. meant to requisition it. There was some scuffling. The local *Hitlerjugend* (Hitler Youth) hissed the members of the S.D. responsible for making the arrangements. The closure of the convent was considered to be an abuse of power.

On 17th October 1943 a class of 14-year-old *Jungmannen* marched from the station to the convent. A band of children confronted them and insulted them, calling them "S.S bastards". A second class arrived on the 27th October, accompanied by experienced teachers from Ilfeld. They issued orders of the day to *Jungmannen*: "We must win over these priest-ridden young people, but don't let's attack religion directly. Let's use our heads and tackle the problem circumspectly."

To start with, the *Napola* invited soldiers from a nearby anti-aircraft battery to play them at football. The result was a goalless draw. The local youth turned out in force, and watched the match in astonishment. After the match, the *Jungmannen* issued a challenge to the youth of

Caricature and scorn in the service of anti-Christian propaganda.

A ceremonial to grip the imagination of the young.

Haselünne. The challenge was accepted, and the result was a 2–0 victory in favour of the *Napola*. The ice was broken. All that was left now was to set up teams representing the district. Then a party was held at the *Napola* on 9th November, and the young people of Haselünne, boys and girls, came in great numbers. The parents had their turn after that. The last barriers were broken down when some young people from the neighbourhood were admitted as pupils to the *Napola*.

The rhythm of *Napola* life was based on the great S.S. and Youth anniversary dates – 30th January, the ceremony of 26th May, the Winter Solstice and, on 9th November, the taking of the oath and the handing over of the daggers.

The celebration of *Julfest* (Yuletide), the S.S. Christmas, brought together all the *Jungmannen* in the fencing room around a fir tree, glittering with a thousand lights. They were there to celebrate, not the birth of Christ, but that of the Child of the Sun, arisen from his ashes at this Winter Solstice. Songs celebrated the struggle between day and night, and the eternal return of life. The *Kommandeur* read aloud the good wishes sent by the 40 other *Napolas*, dispersed over the whole of the Reich territory: Plön, Köslin, Ilfeld, Stuhm, Neuzelle, Putbus, Henge, Rufach and the rest. As each name was called, a boy left the circle of his comrades to light a candle on the huge fir-tree.

There was another ceremony on 24th January. This was the anniversary of the death of Herbert Norkus, the Horst Wessel of the youth, who had been stabbed in Berlin in 1931 by the Socialists at the age of 15. In the evening, the film *Hitlerjunge Quex* was shown, taken from the novel by Schenzinger, itself based on the Norkus story. After the film came the funeral vigil. The drums beat out the funeral call of the Black Order – two long rolls, executed on the tall infantry drums. This litany was suddenly broken by a flourish of trumpets. Then silence invaded the walls of the castle. An adolescent voice rose in the night. Another one responded to it. Then came a third:

"We celebrate this evening the memory of our comrade, Herbert Norkus."

"We do not keep vigil around a cold coffin, but we form closed ranks around a comrade who made the supreme sacrifice."

"He was one who dared before we did. His mouth is silent, but his example lives."

"Many have fallen, but many are born. The world is vast. There is room both for the living and the dead."

Then they sang the song: "A people rises to go on the attack ...".

On 26th May, when night fell, all the *Jungmannen* gathered together on the parade ground, leaving a space between themselves and the buildings. A low platform had been set up there, flanked by torches and

Twenty-six members of the Hitler Youth were killed in street fights with the Communists between 1932 and 1934
(*Snark International*).

banners, serving as an altar for the rite of invocation which was about to be celebrated. On one side stood the young drummers, their infantry long-drums supported against their thighs. On the other side were the young trumpeters, the copper mouthpieces hanging from their hips.

Suddenly, the strident clamour of trumpets breaks the silence. The moan of drums rises in the night, then dies away into the distance. This evening, the young voices, full of anger, are about to evoke the death of Albert Leo Schlageter, one of the first National Socialists:

"Comrades! At this moment throughout the Reich the fanfares call for silence. Men in innumerable columns are meditating piously. The flags are being slowly lowered to salute the shades of those who died for the Fatherland."

"We call upon the memory of the first soldier of the Reich, Albert Leo Schlageter."

"Schlageter was the son of a long line of peasants from the Black Forest. His remains rest there."

Everyone turned towards Munich on 9th November.

"He enlisted as a volunteer and was several times wounded during the War. He fought with the *Baltikum* Volunteer Corps, then in Upper Silesia after the *Diktat* of Versailles.

"When the storm broke in the West in 1923 and when the French troops, violating the law and the peace, invaded the Ruhr, Schlageter fought in the front line. Resistance flared up on all sides. Along with his companions, he paralysed the lines of communications and the redoubts of the enemy by his intrepid actions."

"He fell into the enemy's hands by treachery."

"We, the Youth, we remember his sacrifice. And his example. Like him, we have written a word on our flag: 'Combat'. All that is cowardly and weak must burn. Our law comes from blood and earth. The bright flame shall consume the lukewarm. We shall break all that is rotten and worm-eaten. We shall forge the new Germany."

The 21st June is the shortest night in the year. For the S.S., it is the night of the Sun, warm and redolent. The *Jungmannen* stand around the Solstice bonfire. Limpid voices rise through the darkness:

"The people goes to the people, and the flame to the flame. Rise to the sky, sacred pyre, leap roaring from tree to tree."

The popular Solstice celebrations in the Bavarian Alps.

They started jumping on the ashes, whooping with joy.

The ranks break up. Each approaches the fire to light the torch he is carrying. Then the square re-forms, now full of dancing flames. Afar off on the hills can be seen the lighting up of other fires, saluted by a child's voice reciting:

"See burn the light which shall deliver us from night. Yonder breaks already the dawn of a radiant time in history. The doors of the future are open to those whose hearts burn with love for the Fatherland. See the luminous dots which bring to rebirth the earth still plunged in darkness. The ancient land of the Germans responds to our call and burns with a thousand fraternal fires."

Three *Jungmannen* each carry an oak branch and advance with it towards the fire:

"I sacrifice this branch in memory of the Dead of the War."

"I lay down this branch as a token to the National Socialist revolution."

"I dedicate this branch to the future sacrifices to be enthusiastically made by German youth to the Fatherland."

The choir responds:

"We are fire and the pyre. We are flame and the spark. We are the light and the heat which drive out the dark, the cold and the damp."

Sometimes, the boys and girls of the local *Hitlerjugend* are invited to join the *Jungmannen* around their bonfires for the Solstice celebrations. They all sing in chorus the old popular songs. They grill sausages on the ends of sticks. They joyously see other fires light up afar off, witnessing to the same faith. Everyone is moved that others are participating in the

The return to primitive Germanism.

same celebration. As the flames die down, a certain nostalgia invades their spirits. In the orange light of the fire, the young faces take on a grey appearance. Then, to shake themselves out of their melancholy, they start jumping on the ashes, whooping with joy. Together, they mount a joyous guard until the triumphal appearance of the new sun.

The 9th November is the anniversary of the Feldherrnhalle, the solemn day dedicated to the dead of 1923, when the children gather together in the guardroom of the castle. A low platform is lit by four immense torches, which make the vaulting shimmer. The *Jungmannen* in their last year stand in front of their comrades. Suddenly, the murmuring and the stifled laughter die away. A command rings out: "Stillgestanden!" (Attention!).

The *Kommandeur* makes his appearance, wearing the black uniform of the Order – which has been very little worn since the War began. Around his neck glitters the *Ritterkreuz* (Knight's Cross). His right sleeve flaps in the breeze, reminding the audience of the arm which has been torn to pieces in a battle. Like most of the S.S. who have been wounded, and whose bodies are now only held together by the energy of the individual and artificial limbs, he has been seconded to train the future administrators and officers. He has immense respect from all the boys, which he uses economically, reserving his strictures for the instructors – not the pupils. All eyes are fixed on him.

He speaks: *Jungmannen*, we are met here this evening to participate in the most important ceremony of your young careers. Your comrades in the Edgar Steinbach* year are going to be awarded their *Seitengewehr* (sidearms). The *Kommandeur* then calls each of the boys up by name:

"Henceforth, you will wear on your left side the sword with the motto: *Mehr sein als scheinen* (Be, not seem), which will dominate your life and your death.

Slowly the *Kommandeur* depicts the history of the Swordbearer Knights, who, in the thirteenth century, undertook to conquer Livonia and Estonia, constituting the vanguard of the great Germanic push towards the East. He talks about those men of war, harder than all others, as an example, for they preferred the keen bite of winter to the emollient sweetness of summer; for them no sacrifice was too great.

---

* Edgar Steinbach was a young member of the S.S., killed by the Reds at Chemnitz (Karl-Marx-Stadt) in 1925.

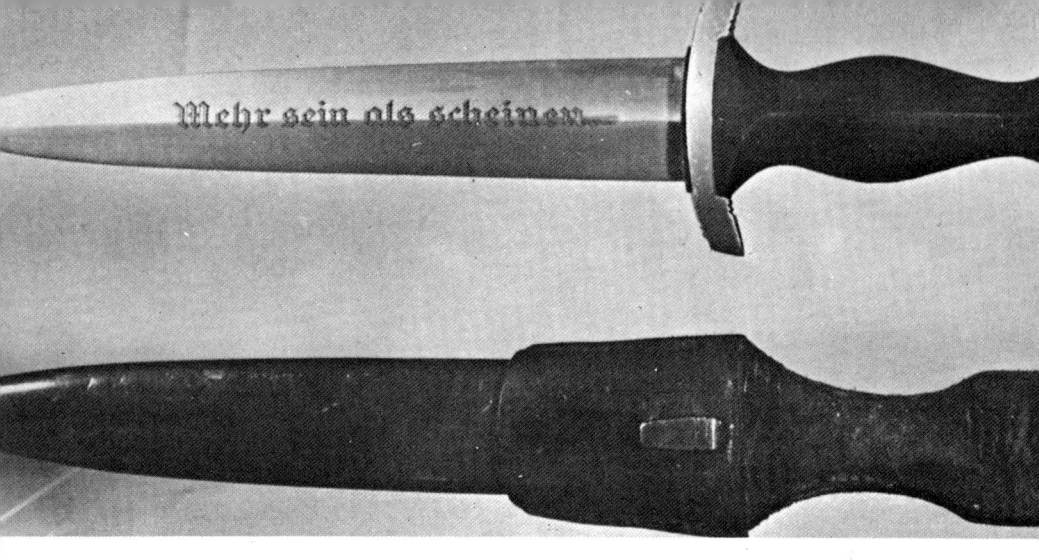

Dagger of the *Napolas*. The shape was similar to that of the S.S. daggers, but this one was carried as a bayonet. The haft has no insignia, but the name of the *Napola* is written above it. On the blade can be read the motto of all the *Napolas*: *Mehr sein als scheinen* (Be, not seem). The instructors' daggers carried the insignia of the *Napola* on the haft and were worn on a chain.

In the silence which follows his last words, the boys' voices ring out under the vaulting:

"Unfurl the standards, gorged with blood, cause the flame to leap to heaven."

Then the postulants form a semi-circle for the vigil which is to last until the sun rises again. At the first light of dawn, their S.S. instructor recalls them to the absolute loyalty which they owe to the Führer by becoming his swordbearers. After enjoining them to leave the ranks of the S.S. if they do not feel themselves capable of dying for the Reich, he hands them their daggers.

Most of the former *Jungmannen* from the *Napolas* were to disappear in the Götterdämmerung in 1945, either killed in combat or summarily executed.

List and year of establishment of the Napolas: 1933: Plön, Potsdam, Köslin. 1934: Berlin-Spandau, Naumburg/Saale, Ilfeld, Stuhm, Oranienstein. 1935: Bensberg, Ballenstedt, Backnang, Rottweil, Klotzsche, Neuzelle, Schulpforta. 1941: Putbus auf Rügen, Loben, Sackau, Vorau, Spanheim, St. Wendel, Henge am Bodensee, Rufach (Alsace), Achern. 1942–1944: Marheim am Donnersberg, Haselünne, Reisen und Wollstein, Annaberg, Mokritz, St. Veit, Göttweig, Hubertendorf u. Türnitz, Colmar-Berg, Raudnitz, Ploschkowitz, Kuttenberg, Wien-Breitensee, Wien-Theresianum, Traiskirchen, Berg-Strechau, Lambach, St. Paul.

CHAPTER 7

The Secret Laboratory of the Millenary Reich

The Ahnenerbe, the S.S. University

In their book, *Le Matin des Magiciens* (The Magicians' Morn), Louis Pauwels and Jacques Bergier wrote:

"It would seem that Germany spent more on research for the *Ahnenerbe* than America did in manufacturing the first atomic bomb. This research ranged from scientific activity in the true sense to the

Insignia worn on the arm by members of the *Ahnenerbe*.

The members of the *Ahnenerbe* wore (on the left) the armband of the *Reichsführer* S.S.'s personal Staff.

study of occult practices, from vivisection practised on prisoners to spying on secret societies. Discussions were held with Skorzeny to organise an expedition with the object of stealing the Holy Grail and Himmler set up a special information department to study the supernatural."

Whether it dealt with expeditions to Tibet or Horbiger's theory of the ice world, the mystery of the *Ahnenerbe* was made all the greater since it was protected by strict secrecy.

On 1st July 1935, Hermann Wirth asked Himmler to set up a learned society under the name *Deutsches Ahnenerbe, Studiengesellschaft für Geistesurgeschichte* (the German Heritage of the Ancestors, a Learned Society concerned with Intellectual Pre-history), which later, on 20th March 1937, became known, more briefly, as the *Ahnenerbe*. Dr. Hermann Wirth was a Dutch university lecturer, who had chosen German nationality and become a volunteer in the 1914 to 1918 War. He was known in university circles for his controversial works on the Middle Ages and Germanic antiquity. He joined the N.S.D.A.P. in 1925, left it in 1926, only to return to it in 1933. Some of his writings, such as: *What is the German Soul?* were not even highly regarded by the Party, since in 1933 Rosenberg silenced him. Dr. Wirth had the great good fortune to meet Himmler at the house of friends of them both at a party during the autumn of 1934. He sketched to him the outline of a learned society with the name *Ahnenerbe*, the object of which would be to study and research Germanic antiquity for the purpose of supporting National Socialist beliefs by scientific proof. The *Reichsführer* S.S. was willingly seduced by the fascination of an idea which lay so close to his own preoccupations, and the Society was accordingly set up in 1935, with the status of a learned society. Himmler also brought in Dr. Walter Darré, the agronomist and the head of *Rusha*. Darré was interested right from the start, and his assistance was of enormous value, since, as he was Minister for Agriculture, he had at his disposal considerable budgetary resources. It was he who paid over the sums necessary for setting up and commissioning the Society. Obviously, the membership contributions were inadequate and, though it is difficult to believe, the S.S. was always short of money and was incapable of making up the difference.

So, the *Ahnenerbe* depended on the S.S. and Darré's Ministry for its life. This was underlined when Wirth and his colleagues took part in the *Green Week* of the Party in 1936, organising an exhibition and lectures.

However, by 1936 differences of opinion were making themselves apparent between Himmler and Darré, causing cracks in the facade of their collaboration. These quarrels were ideological. Darré saw the German as "sedentary", that is, one who was rooted in and strongly attached to his own blood, and the corollary of this was that Germany's role was defensive. At first, Himmler was in agreement with Darré's "static" concept, but later he saw the German, not as "sedentary" but as a Nomadic warrior. This new idea of the Viking, in search of new lands, corresponded more to the ideas of the S.S. and its ambitions to conquer.

Dr. Walter Darré, Minister of Agriculture and racial theoretician, the first patron of the *Ahnenerbe*.

This conceptual difference was to have a profound effect on the future of *Ahnenerbe*. From November 1936 onwards, it was integrated into the *Reichsführer S.S.*'s personal Staff, benefitting from close liaison with Himmler. In February 1937, however, the differences of opinion between Himmler and Darré reached the point of no return, and the *Ahnenerbe* was definitively oriented towards the S.S. Himmler appointed to the Society a special representative, Bruno Galke, whose terms of reference were to cancel out Darré's influence over the Society. One of the first measures to be taken was a gradual exclusion of Wirth, because the latter was too much in league with Darré; Wirth was thus condemned in 1937 to silence, although he continued to be on the S.S. payroll. The man who took his place at the head of the Society had a much larger audience in university circles; Professor Walter Wüst was, in fact, Dean of the University of Munich and the occupant of the chair of the "study of aryan culture and linguistics".

Looking for links with the ancient Nordic civilisation.

Ancient jewels, discovered in Danish tombs and dating from the Roman Iron Age. The two wheels represent a symbolism bound up with the divinities of the heavens and going back to the Bronze Age (*National Museum, Copenhagen*).

Engraved Sanda stone, decorated with solar symbols and a Viking boat, discovered on the island of Gotland, Sweden (Museum of Visby).

After the final elimination of Darré and Wirth, Himmler proceeded on 11th March 1937 to restructure the Society. He felt it necessary to amend its articles of association in order to assert his own authority and to define its aims as he conceived them. He therefore decreed that the *Ahnenerbe* should be integrated into the S.S. This meant that its members became subject to the hierarchy of the S.S. and that the Society was placed under the tutelage of the head of S.S. administration, the *W.V.H.A.* (Central Office of Administration and the Economy),

Oswald Pohl. This decision was charged with menaces for the future, because it was the *W.V.H.A.* and Oswald Pohl who were also responsible for the administration of the concentration camps. The *Ahnenerbe* was thus set on a course which was not appropriate towards the attainment of its ends and which was later to mark it with infamy.

Himmler reserved control for himself with the title of Curator. Effective management was carried out until 1st January 1939 by a trio made up of Bruno Galke, Walter Wüst and Wolfram Sievers. By that date, the integration of the *Ahnenerbe* into the S.S. was complete. Bruno Galke, who was responsible to the Reichsführer S.S. for financial matters, disappeared, and the Society was then managed by Wüst and Sievers alone.

All the members of the Society were bound to adhere to the principles of the S.S.; their work and their results were cloaked in absolute secrecy on pain of death.

The division of power was such that Professor Walter Wüst, titular President since 1937, was responsible for the direction of all the scientific activity, while organisation and finance were in the hands of Wolfram Sievers, who had been Secretary-General of the Society since its foundation and a member of the S.S. since 19th August 1935.

Himmler had certainly found in Sievers one of the most talented administrators in the Reich, of the same mould as Heydrich. He was an organiser and a leader, rather than a scientist. His position in the S.S. was without parallel; he had the privilege of entering Himmler's office and of often eating at his table. He belonged to the *Freundeskreis Himmler* (the Circle of Himmler's Friends) and was admitted to the *Haus der Flieger* (Aviators' House), where the members of the Circle

The swastika in antiquity. Artemis-Hecate, tutelary goddess of wild beasts. A Boeotian amphora of 700 B.C. in the National Museum at Athens.

Ares and Aphrodite – the Museum of Tarquinia.

met and where he cultivated useful contacts among financiers and industrialists; he also had access to the R.S.H.A. (National Security Central Office) and the S.D. (the Security Service).

These contacts were extremely necessary, and were above all used by Sievers to finance the Society. Indeed, after the break with Darré, the *Ahnenerbe* had to find a new source of finance, for Wirth had involved the Society in a considerable amount of expense and claims against it were numerous. Sievers established a foundation of companies which were prepared to make contributions. Other funds were found in the S.D., thanks to Franz Six and Wiepert, who were responsible to the S.D. for university policies and the sciences.

Sievers was cold and distant with his subordinates, and was nicknamed "Gloomy Wolfram". He made himself feared by his sarcasm. He loved poetry and was an expert interpreter of Bach, but both his talents and his ambitions conflicted with Wüst's ideas. The latter had no precise policies; he was a university man and felt himself to be first and foremost a member of the professorial body. In view of all this, he did not have a very good press and, following a quarrel with Sievers concerning prerogatives, he resigned on 12th November 1943. Himmler refused his resignation, but henceforth Wüst was to concentrate rather on his university activities.

Wolfram Sievers was tired and ill; he still had to face the difficulties which had surreptitiously mounted up since 1942. The *Ahnenerbe* was short of manpower and, despite the remarkable organisation, the territorial extension of the services was such that Sievers found it difficult to meet demands. He installed the headquarters of the Society in 1944 at Waischenfeld in Bavaria, while still attempting to maintain to the end communications with Berlin, which grew ever more difficult.

Despite the brilliant defence put up by one of his friends, Wolfgang Hielscher, Wolfram Sievers was condemned by the Tribunal of Nuremberg. He was hanged at Landsberg in 1948. Wüst, on the other hand, who was also condemned to death, was later pardoned.

Himmler had defined the aims of the *Ahnenerbe* in January 1937, in these words:

"It is responsible for carrying out scientific work and research into ancient history. From the scientific and ideological point of view, our job is to study facts, without falsifying them and in an objective fashion.

I wish that every region which has an S.S. organisation should also have a cultural centre, devoted to German greatness and the German past. I would like this cultural centre to be worthy of the people of a great culture, as is seen, for example, in the *Externsteine* of the *Sachsenhain*, near Verden, where 4500 Saxons were massacred. We have rebuilt houses there in a grove, using 4500 prehistoric erratic blocks brought from 4500 Saxon villages. Why did we do this? The answer is simple. We want to show our men and the German people that our past is more than a thousand years old, that we were not a barbarous people without a culture who had to have a culture brought to them from outside. We want our people to be proud of their history, and we want to show that Germany is more eternal than Rome, which is already 2000 years old. The oldest plough that has ever been found was in Germany, made 5000 years ago. Some of the most ancient alphabetic characters, the runes, were invented by Germans and numerous traces of these are found engraved in stone. Arminius was not a nondescript leader of a wild tribe; he conducted a war against Rome with superior military efficiency and his Germans constructed fortifications which were unique for the time.

We want to show every German that the wealth of his land and his culture are the creations of his ancestors. That is the purpose of our scientific and cultural preoccupation with pre-history."

The field of investigation of the *Ahnenerbe* from 1939 onwards was considerably enlarged. Himmler himself was not content to be restricted to ancient history, important though this was for S.S. ideology and mythology. For him, the aim of the *Ahnenerbe* was to confirm, to

On the left: *Sturmann* (Lance-Corporal) – First Class. Armband of the *Ostgruppe* (Eastern Group) – 1938 and dagger, 1933 model.
On the right: *Oberscharführer* (Sergeant-Major), Julius Schreck Regiment (General S.S.).

On the left: sports gear of the Allgemeine S.S. (General S.S.) and the Waffen S.S. (Weapons S.S.). On the right *Scharführer* (Sergeant), brown-shirted uniform of 1935.

Alfred Rosenberg, the National Socialist philosopher, some of whose theories were opposed by Himmler (*U.S. archives*).

modernise and to complement the racist hypotheses of the preceding century. In a strange compound of scientific approach and romantic fervour, he was concerned to re-examine all the foundations of knowledge: "After more than a thousand years of the spiritual dictatorship of Judaic Christianity over Europe, we find it necessary to re-prove everything" were the words of one of his Dutch researchers.

No domain of human knowledge was to remain extraneous to the *Ahnenerbe*, despite Himmler's predilection for German antiquity. The Society was to include more than fifty scientific departments and fifteen or so research commissions. Among the original minds which supported the Society was a large number of university people, more than thirty of them being professors.

Research came under three main headings: *Erbe* (the heritage properly speaking), *Raum* (space) and *Geist* (spirit or mind). In this way, pre-history could co-exist with geopolitics and philosophy with biology.

The *Ahnenerbe* attracted university men or researchers who did not agree with the official ideas of the Party as expressed by Rosenberg. Himmler was far more flexible. He put under his protection all the independent researchers who did not completely go along with the Party line.

Whereas most of the ideologists of National Socialism had considerable mistrust, even hostility, of the university people and intellectuals in general, Himmler rejected and condemned this attitude. He showed evidence of quite a surprising amount of liberalism, and incorporated brilliant university lecturers into the *Ahnenerbe*. Indeed, he made quite a clear line of division between research, on the one hand, and ideological education on the other. The strait-jacket which he

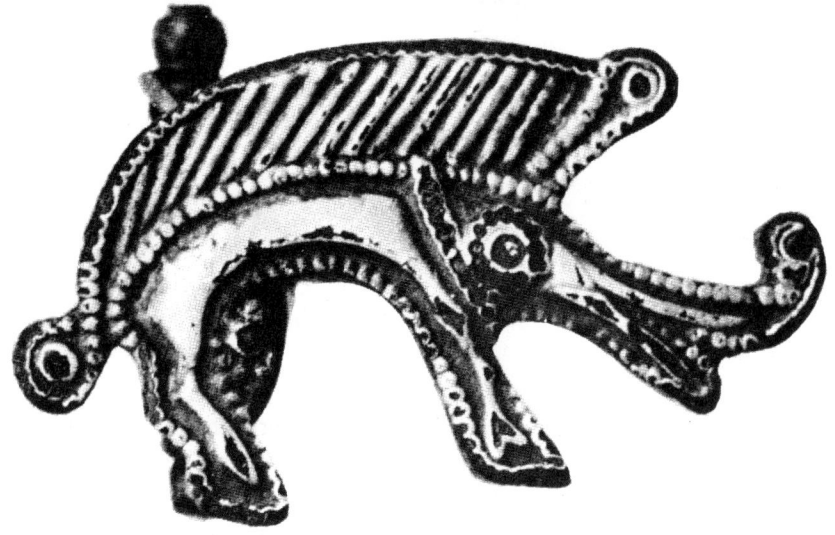

Fibula in the form of a boar, discovered in the *Brudelbrunnen* (boiling fountain), near Bad Pyrmont in Westphalia, Second Century A.D. (*Museum of Bad Pyrmont*).

imposed upon the S.S. made it possible for him to take this calculated risk. At his order, research was to be pursued on the basis of strictly scientific methods. The contract he signed with the researchers, nevertheless, stipulated that, if the results turned out to be contrary to S.S. ideology, they would not be published. This was the least that the Grand Inquisitor could do!

The *Ahnenerbe* invented the technique of study and research groups, made up of researchers coming from different intellectual disciplines, but all working on a common theme. This method is still used today with success in all universities.

Himmler also set up organisations of S.S. students in the university centres to link the *Ahnenerbe* closely to the university faculties. Finally, a university doctorate was an essential qualification for members of the Society; this certainly excluded some who could not overcome this hurdle.

One of the poles of attraction of the research teams was pre-history. Everything was brought to bear to justify – by "digs" and research done on dialect – the existence of a current of superior Germanic culture going back a thousand years.

Dr. Teudt, a former priest, who had a passion for Germanic culture and was famous for his research and theses published in 1929, joined the N.S.D.A.P. in 1933. He also entered the *Ahnenerbe* and became director of the department of *Externsteine* (outcrops), concerned with rich excavations of the cliffs in the Teutoburg Forest, where the Germans of Arminius (sometimes, but wrongly, called Hermann)

S.S. Ring of Loyalty.

crushed the Roman legions of Q. Varus in the year 9 of our era. This place, sacred in German history, was a repository of the culture of the prehistoric age. Dr. Teudt made of it a "territory of ideological interest" for the S.S., where none but members of the Society had the right to carry out excavations.

A further object of these prehistoric researches was to gather together the largest possible amount of information on the oldest Germanic traditions. The S.S. ring with the Death's Head, the symbolism of the runes and the *Julturm* (Yule Tower) were some of the fruits of these labours, carried out to rediscover and revive the past. The S.S. factory at Allach made reproductions of all these objects.

Himmler gave orders in 1938 that all excavations be put in the hands of the *Ahnenerbe*. Their overall direction was to be entrusted to Rolf Höhne, appointed as "Inspector of Excavations". He was personally responsible for the researches carried out at Quedlinburg, in the attempt to find the human remains of Henry the First, the Fowler. His discoveries brought him into conflict with his superiors when the latter received a communication from the medieval history specialist, Carl Erdmann, who strongly contested their authenticity. Subsequently, Wüst and Sievers agreed in finding Höhne's scientific methods suspect. They dismissed him from his functions, and he was replaced by Dr. Hans Schleif.

One of the most prestigious figures in the work of excavation was Herbert Jankuhn, a close friend of the pre-history team leader,

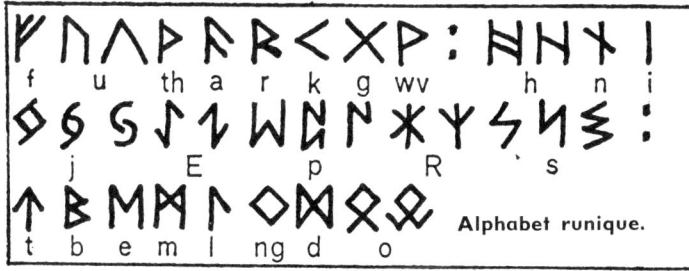

The runic alphabet.

Professor Lothigsdorf. He was responsible for the excavations at Haithabu, and these provided the Society with one of its greatest successes. Jankuhn was later promoted to be director of an institute of ancient history at Kiel and given a university chair. Although the results of his researches were shelved at the start of the War, Jankuhn brought out in 1943 a provisional report of great scientific value on the excavations at Haithabu. He found that Haithabu, in Schleswig, represents the end of the defensive wall built in the 9th Century by King Godfred to defend the Danes against incursions from the Carolingians (the descendants of Charlemagne).

Once War had broken out, the *Ahnenerbe's* researches and work were to some extent laid to rest. Himmler took precautions, however, to maintain a skeleton staff so that the work of the departments could be resumed as soon as peace returned.

Improvisation was the keynote at the start of the War. Sievers had to find new forms of activity in tune with the new requirements of the moment. These new activities, principally concerned with medical research, were not directly conducted by the *Ahnenerbe* – which was content to give some technical support. This was just as well because, along with traditional forms of work, undertakings were developed which were at best suspect, and at worst notoriously criminal.

One of the most alarming figures among the researchers was Professor Hirt, occupant of the Chair of Anatomy at the University of

A neo-pagan demonstration in the Olympic Stadium in Berlin.

Professor Hirt, occupant of the Chair of Anatomy at the University of Strasbourg. He is seen here in the uniform of *S.S. Hauptsturmführer* (Captain).

Strasbourg, where S.S. students were particularly numerous. With Himmler's support, Professor Hirt brought together at the concentration camp in Auschwitz a collection of skulls for the purpose of making anthropomorphic measurements. The subjects chosen were all people who had been condemned to death. Later he went personally to the front to study the behaviour of combatants as a function of their attachment to one or the other racial category.

Another anatomical specialist, Professor Beger, collected skeletons of different races; these included those of a number of political commissars of the Red Army of Eurasian origin, who were put to death in cold blood for the purpose.

Professor Ernst Schäfer was one of the oldest members of the Society, and before the War had already acquired some renown in Germany for his journeys to Tibet. He was commissioned by Himmler to select for military use a race of horses of the Steppes which would be particularly resistant to cold temperatures.

Other research took place in the camps and doctors used these to aid their study of diseases.

Sigmund Rascher was one of the doctors with the most sinister reputation. He carried out medical experiments on detainees who had been condemned to death. Supplied with a permit from Himmler, he went to Dachau, along with his wife, and succeeded in obtaining from the Luftwaffe the use of a pressurised chamber to carry out experiments on the effects of decompression. A doctor in the Luftwaffe, Dr. Ruff,

Himmler never lost his passion for the work of the *Ahnenerbe*.

and his assistant, Dr. Romberger, who had both been made responsible for looking into the proper use of Army equipment, joined Rascher and his assistant, Welt, at Dachau. The first experiments took place between March and April 1941. Romberger was present at two experiments. As these were fatal to both the prisoners, Dr. Romberger refused to take part in any more. He referred the matter to his superior, Dr. Ruff, who demanded that the pressure chamber be returned. It was sent back to Berlin on 23rd May 1941.

Rascher then bent his attentions to the problems of survival in cold conditions, again on the basis of human guinea pigs. He was able to benefit from the confidence shown in him by Himmler up to the day when it was noted that his wife and he were nothing but dangerous charlatans. The pitiless law of the S.S. was brought to bear on the couple. The wife was imprisoned at Ravensbrück and executed in March 1945, whereas her husband was killed in his cell at Buchenwald on 7th April 1945.

However, it must not be thought that all the medical studies carried out within the framework of the *Ahnenerbe* were of this terrible and fantastic nature. One of the benefits they provided was the development of haemostatic and coagulant products, which did much to help the wounded men in the Wehrmacht and the Waffen S.S.

Another principal sector of scientific research, that of secret weapons, fell under the authority of the *Ahnenerbe* in 1944. Up to the middle of that year, Werner V. Braun, who directed operations at Peenemünde, seemed to be faithful to the Wehrmacht, although he was an S.S. officer. He had even been arrested by the Gestapo once. However, after 20th July 1944 Himmler took control of the rocket programme. By that time, the German people as a whole were laying all their hopes on secret weapons. It is well known that the V1 and the V2 were developed too late to avoid the ultimate defeat.

All these activities, that went on in parallel, never impeded the *Ahnenerbe* from pursuing its researches, nor did they lessen the *Reichsführer*'s interest in them.

Once the War had entered its most critical phase and Himmler was overwhelmed by the load of responsibility which gave him very little time to do anything but attend to his police and military functions, he still made time to read the *Ahnenerbe* reports attentively. He used to say that it was his only real pleasure and his only real relaxation. He wrote a long and critical letter on 17th August 1944 to Professors Wüst and

Wolfram Sievers, resulting from a communication he had received about ancient Germanic customs. One or two passages from this correspondence will better enable us to understand the intellectual and quasi-religious motivations of this enigmatic personage:

"Having read your letter", Himmler wrote, "I should like to make the following remarks concerning the customs and the history of German law in respect of the tombs of the ancestors and the marriage stones. In general, I think that legal ceremonies, among which, of course, marriages were one of the most important, were formerly carried out on the tombstone of the collective vault of the extended family. This squares with the practice of our still more ancient forebears and their belief that the dead participated in the whole life of their descendants, who were obligated to answer to them for everything.

You have written in your report: 'Tradition relates that marriages were solemnised on the tombstone during the Thirty Years War.' This is quite possible because during the Thirty Years War, at a time when the villages were emptied and the peasants went to live in the forests, the ancestors' tomb, or at least a rock which looked like it, represented the seat of justice.

Your report further states: 'Another tradition relates that girls who sat there at midnight usually found a husband, once they had satisfied certain obligations.'

In this connection I wish to mention a custom of our own time, and one which was certainly in use around the year 1930. A girl in Kiel had a child, and when she was asked who the father was, replied that hers

A Germanic cauldron, illustrated in the book by Jörg Lechler: *Ein germanisches Kultfest vor 3000 Jahren*, Leipzig 1935.

Reconstruction at Stadingen of an ancient Germanic village where plays were presented on a natural scale. These performances drew considerable crowds.

was a 'child of the stone'. When they questioned her further, she told them about the following old custom. If there was a girl in the village of an age to be married who had not yet found a husband, she used to go out on a moonlit night (the new moon) with her father and the local peasants. She used to lie on the ancestors' tomb, and the peasants would stand in a large circle around her, facing outwards. The father would previously have made an arrangement with a man living in the village – that is, someone who formed part of the blood community. This man then left the circle, climbed on the tomb and mated with the girl; sexual intercourse actually took place on the tomb.

The meaning of this custom is as follows: no good blood must die without having been fruitful. But the child must be conceived from a man of good blood, belonging to the village blood community. What took place was no act of licence; on the contrary, it took place in sight of the ancestors and on their tomb.

Something similar can be seen on your page 26, where it is shown that newly-married couples had to visit the tomb of their ancestors at the time of the new moon. Perhaps the new moon is, either according to belief or in reality, a period which is particularly favourable to fertility. Research on wild animals would throw more light on this point, as would also experience gained from the rearing of domestic animals and from zoology in general."

Himmler goes on in the same strain for a couple more pages. It must not be thought that he consisted of two different persons, one a peaceful bookworm, discoursing on things of the spirit and, the other, an implacable political policeman. His personality was all one. He was, essentially a Caliph or a Grand Inquisitor, ready to take any action to impose his faith on others.

The secret catalogue of the undertakings and works of the Ahnenerbe.

Brochures called *Deutsches Ahnenerbe*, started in July 1935, in association with the publishers, Koehler und Amelang of Leipzig, which went on until April 1938.

The *Nordland* magazine, started in 1935.

The *Germanien* magazine, published from March 1936 onwards, in collaboration with the *Vereinigung der Freunde germanischer Vorgeschichte* (the Association of Friends of Germanic Pre-history). This learned publication had a certain amount of success. The number of its subscribers went up from 2000 in 1936 to 12,500 in 1937. It ceased to appear in July 1943.

Establishment of the publishing house of *Ahnenerbe-Stiftung* at Berlin in April 1938. Its work was directed, from the summer of 1939, by Friedhelm Kaiser, the vice-president of the *Ahnenerbe*.

Setting up in the Low Countries of the magazine *Hammer* in October 1940, directed by Hans Schneider.

Excavations on the *Externsteine* (in the Teutoburg Forest), undertaken in 1936 by Dr. Teudt.

An expedition to the Near East in 1938, headed by Franz Altheim and Erika Trautmann.

Taking over the Pre-history Museum at Kiel by Herbert Jankuhn in 1938.

Excavations carried out on the Viking site of Haithabu, to the south of Schleswig, between the spring of 1938 to September 1939, by Herbert Jankuhn.

Taking over in 1938 of the Observatory of München-Grünwald, directed by Philipp Fauth.

The first expedition to Tibet (April 1938 to August 1939), under the direction of Dr. Ernst Schäfer, including filming.

The archives of the *Deutsche Volkserzählung*, (a society which collected popular German stories and recitations) were confided to the *Ahnenerbe* in 1938.

The Religious Ethnography Institute at Salzburg was integrated with the

Ahnenerbe in September 1938.

In 1938 the Library of Lionel Feuchtwanger, sequestrated by the Gestapo, was acquired.

The House of Nature at Salzburg came under the *Ahnenerbe* control in 1939.

The *Ahnenerbe* was given supervision on 25th March 1939 of the archaeological excavations and the protection of buildings of historical interest in the Protectorate of Bohemia/Moravia.

In May 1939, the Association of German Biologists was dissolved and replaced by a *Reichsbund für Biologie* (Reich Association for Biology) under the aegis of the *Ahnenerbe*.

First experiments in the anti-cancer campaign of Dr. Sigmund Rascher at Dachau Camp, June 1939.

Excavations at Karnburg, in Austria, undertaken during the summer of 1939.

Excavations at Unter-Wisternitz, near Nikolsburg (Czechoslovakia), carried out by Assien Bohmers in July 1939.

The setting up on 15th September 1939 at Bolzano of an official organisation for German emigration, directed by Wilhelm Luig.

Medical experiments for military purposes were not the monopoly of S.S. doctors. We see here Dr. Holst, of the Luftwaffe, doing an experiment on resistance to cold at Dachau (*Ullstein*).

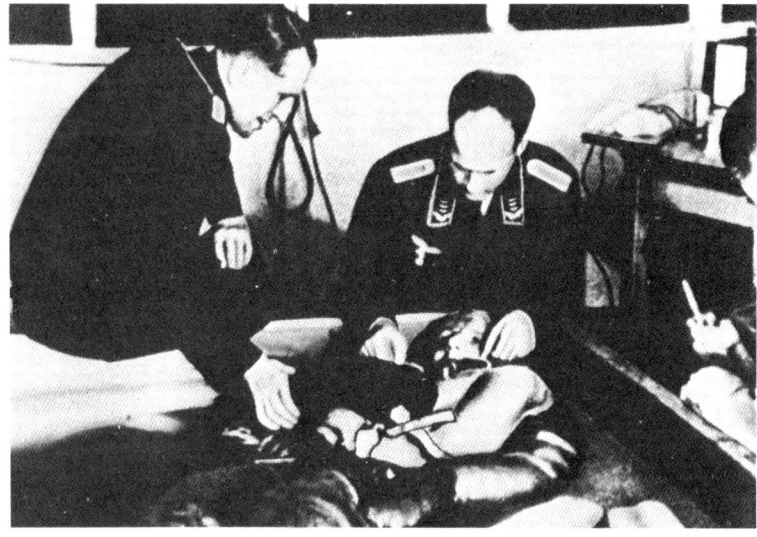

On 16th December 1939, Heinrich Harmjanz was appointed by Himmler to be *General-Treuhänder* (Trustee-General) of the cultural heritage of that part of Poland which was taken over by the Reich.

The *Ahnenerbe* was represented on the Committee of German Archives in Estonia and Latvia (December 1939).

Excavations at Biskupice, in Poland, from spring 1940 to summer 1942.

Work by Hans Schleif in the excavations at Olympia, in Greece, autumn 1940.

The foundation towards the end of 1940 of the *Volksche Werkgemeenschap* (Society of Community Studies) in the Netherlands, directed by Hans Schneider.

Excavations in Slovakia, undertaken in September 1940 under the direction of Kurt Willvouseder and Lothar Zotz.

An agreement concluded in spring 1941 with the Reich Minister of Education concerning the university policy towards pre-history.

The foundation in May 1941 at Salzburg of the *Reichsbund für Karst und Höhlenforschung* (the Reich Association for Karst Exploration and Speleology), under the aegis of the *Ahnenerbe*.

Excavations carried out at the Croat fortress of Sarval, undertaken during the summer of 1941 by R. R. Schmidt.

Work of the Cultural Commission of the *Ahnenerbe* in South Tyrol (Italy) from autumn 1941 to August 1942.

Prehistoric excavations in Serbia, 1941. The *Ahnenerbe* was given the monopoly of these excavations in February 1942.

The setting up in 1942 of a German Institute at the Hague (Netherlands).

The protection of prehistoric tombs and sites in Southern Russia, initiated during the summer of 1942 under the direction of Herbert Jankuhn.

Archaeological research in Caucasia, undertaken in the summer of 1942 under the direction of Dr. Ernst Schäfer.

The *Ahnenerbe* was given control of the Anthropos Museum at Brno (Czechoslovakia) in the autumn of 1942 under the direction of Hermann Schwabedissen.

The *Ahnenerbe* was given control of the *Haus Germanien* (Germanic Institute) at Hildesheim in January 1944 under the direction of Peter Paulsen.

CHAPTER 8

The Black Order

Himmler Speaks

1. **Principles of the S.S. Order** (a speech made to the generals of the S.S. at Poznan on 4th October 1943.)

"We have subjected ourselves to the law of the élite. We have set up rigorous criteria for the body, the character and the mind. We have always selected the highest and abandoned the lowest. As long as we have the strength necessary to maintain this principle, this Order will remain healthy. When we no longer apply to ourselves this fundamental law, the law of elimination and severity, at that time we shall be condemned to death and we shall perish like every other human organisation. That is why we must, at all times and in all places, remind ourselves of the principles: blood, élite and endurance.

This is the law of nature: what is hard is good, what is strong is good, what proceeds from the struggle for existence, at the level of the body, the character and the mind, is good from the point of view of endurance.

After the War, we shall really build up our Order, that Order to which we imparted its most important principles ten years before the War. We shall continue, we the veterans, for twenty years after the War, so that a tradition can be established, a tradition that will last for

The law of the Black Elite.

thirty, thirty-five or forty years – a whole generation. Then our Order will be young and strong, revolutionary and active, in its march into the future. It will be able to fulfil its duty and provide the Germanic people with an élite. This élite will unite this people and the whole of Europe. It will keep them together. It will produce the leaders to direct industry, agriculture, politics and the activities of the mind. This élite must be sufficiently strong and vigorous so that each generation can, without argument, offer up two or three sons per family on the field of battle without exhausting the torrent of Germanic blood.

The fundamental qualities of the S.S. order

"I should now like to speak about the most important qualities which I laid down years ago for this Order and for the *Allgemeine S.S.* (General S.S.), the crucible of the Order. In this fifth year of the War, these qualities are of the highest importance.

First, there is loyalty. God be praised, we have never had a single case of treason in our ranks. The following is the main line of conduct. If an S.S. leader were to become faithless towards the Führer or towards the Reich, if only in thought, you must do what is necessary to enable this man to leave the Order. We will do what is necessary so that he is removed from life itself. I have already said, and I repeat it once more today, everything can be pardoned; but one thing is unpardonable among us Germans, and that is disloyalty.

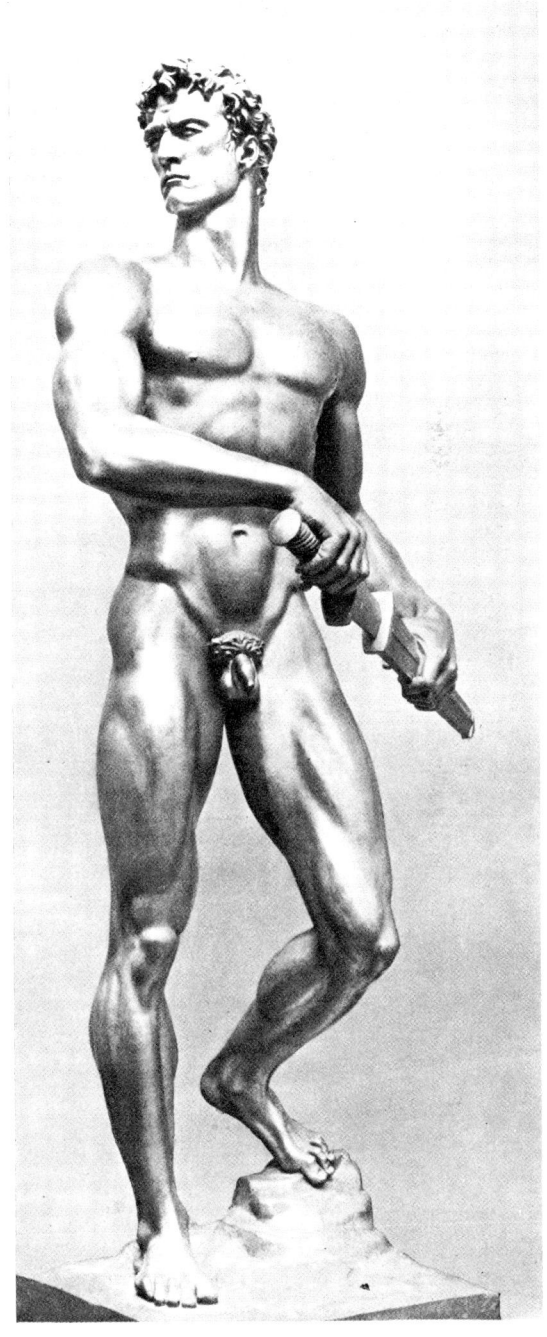

Strength. Statue by Arno Brecker for the *Zeppelinfeld* (Zeppelin Field) at Nuremberg.

The last appearance in public of the *Blutfahne* (Flag of Blood) of 1923 at the funeral of Gauleiter Wagner in 1944.

Second comes obedience. Obedience is required of the soldier from the morning to the evening. It is easily obtained from the lower ranks. The problem is more difficult at the higher levels in the State, the Party or the Army. For us, though it may well be obvious and natural that those called upon to carry out orders should obey, it is still more natural that the leaders of the S.S. and, in particular, the body of generals, should present an example of unreserved obedience.

If one of them should consider that an order is based on an error by his superior, he has of course the right and duty to discuss it with him and to present his reasons courageously and frankly. But, from the moment when this superior confirms the order in question, it must be carried out, not only to the letter, but also in the spirit. He who executes the order does so as a faithful representative of authority. If, however, he considers that he cannot take the responsibility of executing the order that has been given, he must say so openly and request to be released from the obligation. In most cases, the order will be once more confirmed. In that case, it must be carried out, in spite of everything. If it is not done, the superior will rightly consider that the nerves of his subordinate are no longer as strong as they should be, that he has become too weak; in that case, he will retire him.

Thirdly, courage. I scarcely need to mention this quality, since our leaders and our men are so courageous. What I want to talk about is

The *Schellenbaum* (Belltree) was carried at the head of an S.S. brass band.

The Chinese hat, of Turkish origin, was introduced into Prussia in the 18th Century via Poland and Austria. Originally, it was a command emblem of the Janissaries (*Illustration by Mollo*).

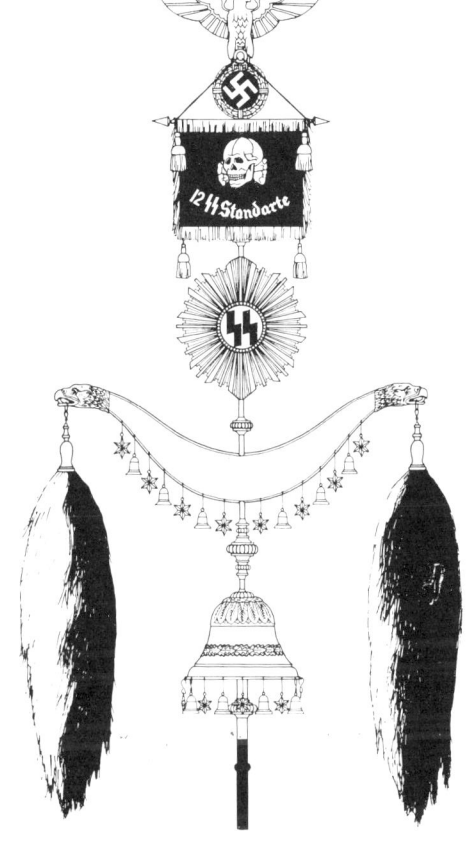

another courage, intellectual and moral courage. I know many of our best S.S. leaders who would never hesitate to attack a bunker or a stronghold, but who sometimes criticise a subordinate. When this subordinate has been posted, they pretend to be surprised: 'What a dirty trick! I can't understand it. I'm going to talk to Berlin about it. It must be another mistake on the part of the personnel department.' It would have been fairer to have had the courage to say: 'I'm not satisfied with you, so you'll have to leave us.'

Another aspect of courage is faith. We must not allow anyone else on this earth to be superior to us in this respect. Faith wins battles, faith leads to victories. Pessimists, and those who lose faith, must leave our ranks. The position they occupy is quite indifferent, no matter whether it is in the State, the Waffen S.S. or the Security Police. Weak men,

Guard on the *Königsplatz* at Munich.

those who have no faith, will have to leave us. We do not want them.

I now come to a fourth quality which is very rare in Germany, loyalty to truth. The most evil feature throughout the War system is the lack of truth in minutes and reports which juniors submit to their superiors. These minutes and these reports constitute the basis for every decision. I estimate that, in a number of fields, 85% of the reports are partially false, whether they concern personnel, equipment, promotion or decorations.

In time of war, as in time of peace, the S.S. will no longer sign written contracts. A word given and a handshake will have the force of a contract.

When we sign contracts, we must keep them, even though a particular contract may have been concluded with a scoundrel. If I say in Poland that every person who denounces a Jew will receive half the latter's fortune, this promise must be kept. For example, if a Jew possesses 12,000 Marks and a secretary or corporal chooses to pocket the 6000 Marks due to the Pole who has denounced the Jew, giving him instead only 400 Marks, then he violates the promise given by the organisation as a whole and destroys the confidence which is due to it. This sort of thing must never happen. When we give our word, it must be kept. We must behave ourselves in this way throughout the whole world, and in this way we, the S.S., will win faith and confidence for Germany. Those who do not turn to the authorities will turn to us.

Nuremberg Congress, September 1934.

Don't mince words with guilty persons.

It must be impossible for any member of the Order, even though he may be in the police, to break his word once given, for that word is sacred.

I now come to justice. Justice does not have to be formal, but it is rather the spirit of justice. Now, we have to admit that justice is not always practised among us. As you know, I examine all the sentences passed by the tribunals of the Order against S.S. leaders, and I study the way my officers judge each other. You know the proverb that dog does not eat dog. We have a lot to learn from the old Prussian Army. An organisation is healthy as long as it retains its capacity to purge itself. Instead of the will to purge ourselves of harmful elements, which still obtained in William I's army, we have a lawyer mentality. We no longer talk about the elimination of a weak member, but we make excuses. In this way, we are protecting in advance a fault that we may ourselves commit, in a similar way, in the future. I want you, generals of the S.S., in your capacity as judges, to be aware more closely of what is going on, so that you do not suppress it. The higher the rank, the more severely must the guilty person be punished.

When a decision has been taken, I'm always curious to know who has made the decision. Not only does this allow us to reward undistinguished people; it has the positive advantage that we sometimes discover someone who has not yet done anything to attract our

1935 Congress.

attention. In this way we may discover in our ranks someone of intelligence and thus open the way to a talented man, perhaps to a genius. If the decision has not been a good one, then I do not wish you commanders to cover up, without good reason, a mistake that has been made. We must have enough authority to enable us to recognise that we have sometimes made a mistake. With our work, we can tolerate a certain percentage of wrong decisions. Finally, I want ministerial officials not to hide behind anonymity, as the Jews did in the past.

The next point I would like to stress is integrity. I can say this in this closed hall, before this restricted gathering; we have become a corrupt people. However, we should not take that too tragically, nor do we need to. It is said that the Finns are an honest people. Well, do you know why they are honest? It is not because they have extraordinary qualities of character, but because their laws have for the last three hundred years laid down that anyone who steals one Finnish Mark will have his hand cut off. This is what has made that people an honest people. We must see a thing clearly and begin with ourselves. We shall never be able to master the pest of corruption within ourselves unless we pursue it like men possessed, without pause or respite, degrading the guilty

Himmler congratulates S.S. *Sturmbannführer* (Major) Kempka, Hitler's personal chauffeur, on his promotion.

party, taking from him his position and his rank and discrediting him before his inferiors. What we call corruption is not so considerable in our ranks anyway. We shall highlight all cases that come before the tribunals without respect of persons.

In the matter of commodities which have been in such short supply since 1936 and 1937, silk, stockings, chocolate, coffee, the temptation is great and we don't want to be executioners. I know you can still buy these things in France, in Belgium and elsewhere, on the black market. A lot of people see nothing criminal in this, but I can assure you that, when the War is over and things are normal again in Germany, these goings-on will be very severely dealt with by the S.S.

As for the veterans of our movement, if they make mistakes, they must be held responsible and punished; if their offence is serious, they must even pay with their lives. We shall not give them any special privileges, because if we punish one, and let the others know, eighty other veterans will be saved. But if we once say: 'Oh, he's an old Nazi or an old S.S. leader; we can't sentence him', then we shall become guilty *vis-à-vis* the other eighty, and the whole of our organisation will crumble."

2. The Need to be Pitiless (speech delivered on 14th October 1943 at Bad Schachen, on the banks of Lake Constance, to the *Gruppenführer* S.S. (Major-Generals).

"Thanks to the measures taken since 1933, the number of criminal offences has been constantly reduced. In 1941 we registered the smallest number of criminal cases known since the foundation of the Third Reich, although we had been at war for three years. The reason for this is the new laws which have been passed in the Third Reich, making it permissible to eliminate or put out of action those elements among us that are criminal. Elimination by death is applied more often and more brutally than it was in the past. Being put out of action involves either imprisonment or internment in a concentration camp.

You can be sure that, if those 40,000 political criminals and those 70,000 associates or professional criminals were at present at liberty, our security would be menaced. But as we have them under close arrest and as, I may say in passing, we use their strength to a good purpose for war ends, obtaining from them many millions of working hours for armaments, our situation from the security point of view has improved from year to year.

S.S. responsible for mounting guard at the Dachau Camp, 1938.

In the matter of the struggle against Communism within, I note that our people and our workers are, since the War began, of such extraordinary honesty and they so faithfully accomplish their duty that we have no difficulties in this respect.

Another question is that of defeatism in intellectual and well-off circles. You must have read in the press that Chairman of the Council Z or Industrialist Y have been judged, condemned to death by a people's court and shot because they have given vent to defeatist opinions. On my soul and conscience, I insist that such judgements must be made public.

If those same defeatist sentiments were held by a young man of twenty, this would be of no importance. It could be that he is basically all right and only needs to be re-educated. If, on the other hand, the same thing is said by a man of mature age, holding a position of dignity, he must come ruthlessly under the laws of war and lose his head. This must be known, because it is the only manner of regaining an advantage for the nation from a broken life, and of making thousands of gossips see reason. That is why I have always been an advocate of hard and pitiless punishment, wherever it is necessary. Such chastisement is not made to remain secret. It is the only way of attaining an educational end.

The enemies of National Socialist doctrine and of Germany rise against us throughout the world. The Jews are always the first. Now there are people who maintain that we have no right to attack Jews in this way. To that argument, gentlemen, I can only make the following objection. It is well known that Germany had no anti-Semitism during the years 1917 to 1918. She cannot be reproached for this. Nevertheless, the Jew opposed the Germany of that time with all his strength and did all he could to make us lose the War. The same has been true today. Every movement whose aim has been to disorganise Germany in order to rob us of victory was led by a Jew, whether he was a democrat, a Spartacist, or a member of a Soviet of workers or soldiers.

Heydrich, the pitiless. Specimen of his handwriting (below).

Members of the S.D. interrogate Jews in the Warsaw ghetto.

A second main enemy is Freemasonry. There are people who say that Freemasonry is an inoffensive organisation that has no need to be dissolved. The fact is that it was Freemasons who planned, prepared for and carried out the events of November 1918. Freemasons are like Jews and Communists. The same goes for the democratic and plutocratic States. They all hate us. They hated Germany in 1918, and they still hate us. To the enemies I have just mentioned – Judaism, Freemasons, Bolshevists, democrats and plutocrats, I would now add to the list the Christian churches which meddle in politics. On the one hand, there is Protestantism, which constitutes in England a true State Church. On the other hand, there is Catholicism, with its own ideas, plans and its arrangements to take over power.

We punish severely citizens of a foreign country who have relations with German women and girls. Every case which is reported and confirmed involves the appearance of the woman in question before a competent law court. If the complicity of the woman is proved, that is, if she has provoked the foreigner in question – and I am thinking particularly of Poles and Russians – the man is locked up in a concentration camp for the whole of his life. In very severe cases, he is condemned to death by hanging and immediately executed on the spot. This may appear very severe, but I am convinced that we owe this severity to ourselves and to our people. If large quantities of foreign

Irma Grese became an S.S. *Hilferin* (Auxiliary) at the age of 18 and was appointed to look after the women's quarters in the camps of Auschwitz and Belsen. She was hanged at the age of 21, on 12th December 1945. She denied up to the end that she had ever ill-treated detainees, as had been alleged.

blood were to mingle with ours, this would constitute a reduction in the value of our greatest possession – our blood.

It is obvious that the cross-matings of different people will always produce some individuals of a good racial type. I think that in such cases we should withdraw these children from their environment and bring them here, even if we have to remove them by force and kidnap them. Such a measure as this may appear strange to our European sensitivity, and some will say: 'How can you be so cruel as to take a child from its mother?' To this question, I would reply: 'How can you be cruel enough to leave a brilliant future enemy on the other side of the border who will later kill your sons and your grandsons?' Either we are going to recuperate this superior blood to use it for our own purposes or we shall destroy that blood. But we cannot take the responsibility of leaving that blood to the other side so that our enemies may have capable leaders. It would be a stab in the back for the present generation to hesitate to take a decision and to leave it to our descendants.

Killers drawn from the S.D. *Einsatzgruppen* in action. The officers came from the police forces. The men consisted partly of policemen and partly of members of the Waffen S.S. who had been dismissed for grave disciplinary offences. There were 1500 men in all, and they were given the choice between the scaffold and joining the organisation.

The war to be conducted against Russia has a particular character by reason of the cruelty with which the Slavs wage it. That is why it is necessary to be pitiless in regard to the man who does not do his duty, his punishment ranging from deprivation of rank to death.

We are faced by an adversary who applies the laws of war with Slav cruelty both within his own ranks and against us. I am of the opinion that we must oppose him with the type of defence which is native to us, a Germanic defence, which makes us as hard as the men on the other side, hardened as they are by their political commissars. The Middle Ages left us a lovely slogan: *Ehre ist Zwang genug* (Honour impels). I consider that this motto is useful for us Teutons and Germans. What we have to do, we shall do.

I think we should adopt the rules of the former Prussian Army. When an officer was shown to be incapable, he was dismissed with the rank of captain. Frederick the Great used to say in such circumstances: 'He has not been successful.' I have adopted this system for the S.S., according to which it is perfectly possible to degrade a non-commissioned officer or a commissioned officer who has not done his duty, before all his battalion. This stripping of rank is carried out without mercy. We have no obligations to spare the feelings of individuals, only to protect the interests of the nation."

3. **The Tasks Ahead of Us** (Extracts from Himmler's speech to the S.S. generals at Poznan on 4th October 1943).

"The future has a very heavy responsibility in store for us. A war has to be won spiritually, by will-power and by the spirit, for material victory is only a symbol. The man who loses hope, faith and the will to resist is in a state of surrender. That man wins the battle who goes on fighting for an hour after the armistice has been declared. We must show our ardour and our obstinacy. We must show our foes that we, the S.S., are harder and juster, and that we never give up. In these fifth and sixth years of the War, we shall be those who retain our poise, who do not give way to gloom and who are ever ready for the most outright action when necessary. This we shall do. We shall be an example to others, and they will draw strength from seeing us. We must have the will-power – and we have – to eliminate all those who, in Germany, for any reason whatsoever, refuse to partake in the communal effort. We must eliminate them calmly and with sang-froid. It is better to shoot some than to engage in a general collapse. As long as our minds are in a proper state, we shall win this War, in harmony with the laws of history and nature, because we represent the World's highest values, and we incarnate the highest and most powerful values that can be found in nature.

When the War has been won, then our work will just be beginning. However, we do not yet know when the end of the War will be. It may well be that it will last for a long time yet. I have already said today that, at the moment when the armistice is signed and peace returns, none among us will be able immediately to enjoy the luxury of going off to sleep in peace. We shall remain at our posts – others can sleep. I shall retain the whole of the S.S. on the alert, in order to begin together the reconstruction of Germany.

We shall enact special laws to enable us to remain mobilised for years, and we shall reform the Waffen S.S. units. Once peace has been

The conscience of the new Reich. Himmler was a top-grade organiser with an unbending will. He was, at the same time, one of the most enigmatic personages of the Third Reich. The most faithful among the faithful, he considered himself to be absolved from his oath as soon as Hitler decided to perish in Berlin, surrounded by the foe. He attempted to negotiate a separate peace in the West, and then committed suicide after his capture by the British troops.

Badge worn on sports gear.

finally signed, we shall begin our great work for the future. We shall colonise territories and we shall teach the laws of the S.S. Order to the young people. I consider it necessary for the life of our people to teach our grandsons to enter into this same life and to understand the difficulties of their ancestors. There can be no doubt that it will be our Order, the racial élite of the German people, which will have the greatest progeny. In twenty or thirty years, we must truly become the directing force for the whole of Europe. If the S.S. and the peasants together largely colonise the East with revolutionary fervour and without hedging or mincing matters, then in twenty years our ethnic frontiers will be advanced for five hundred kilometres to the East.

I have today asked the Führer for permission, on behalf of the S.S., when we have fulfilled our duty and our War tasks, to be given the right of holding that defence frontier which will constitute the outer boundary of Germany in the East. No one shall take this privilege from us. We shall there be able to drill our young people in the use of arms and we shall dictate our law to the East. We shall advance ever further, and we shall reach the Urals. I hope that our generation will be able to carry out this work, that every man will have fought in the East and that every division will be able to pass one winter in the East every two or three years. In this way, we shall never weaken, we shall not have among us mere uniform-wearers, who only join up in time of peace because the

"We will never weaken." *Himmler.*

black uniform is more elegant. Every man who joins the S.S. must know that, at any moment, he may be mortally wounded. He must pledge himself not to go dancing every couple of years in Berlin or to have a good time at the Munich Carnival, but he must be at his post in the icy winter of the Eastern frontier. In this way, we shall have a healthy élite, ready for everything.

We are going to create the chance for the Germanic people and for Europe as a whole, directed by the Germanic people, to build an ordered Europe which will, for generations, be able to fight victoriously against all Asiatic aggression. We do not know when this will take place. What we do know is that there is in existence a yellow horde consisting of a billion and a half men. Facing them is the Germanic people in unity, with its two hundred and fifty to three hundred million men, making up, together with the other European peoples, a total of six hundred to seven hundred million men on a territory for military exercises extending to the Urals. We shall then be able to impose our will on Asia. Woe to us if the Germanic people cannot win this battle! It will be the end of beauty, of culture and of creative thought on this earth. We struggle for that future and we shall maintain the heritage of

On the left: *Standartenführer* (Colonel) of the S.D. Armband of an *Abteilungsleiter* (Divisional Commander) on the *Reichsführer* S.S.'s Staff. On the right: *Scharführer* (Sergeant) of the S.D. Helmet model 1933.

Military evening dress:
On the left:
Hauptsturmführer (Captain) of the *S.S. Reichsführun*
(1943).
On the right:
Unterscharführer (Lance-Sergeant).

our ancestors. We know the face we want to give to that future. For this reason, we are more fanatical than ever, our belief is stronger than ever, we are more obedient and we are more upright than ever, for this is our duty."

At the very moment when Himmler was giving vent to these inspired words, the Order on which he was calling with all the force of his fanaticism was withering as a result of its excessive growth.

The S.S. was the victim of the morbid hunger of its leader. The *Reichsführer* had long since forgotten the prudent selective methods that he recommended in 1937. The S.S. was no longer an élite minority. No longer did it seek quality before anything else. The more its tentacles stretched out, the more its activities were diversified and the more its power increased, the less homogenous and coherent it became. Despite the police system installed in its heart to supervise, control and punish, this immense body was disintegrating into cliques and factions. Having consecrated an essential part of its activity to the least excusable tasks of policing, repression and extermination, the S.S. was now stripped of the character, of a demanding new aristocracy, to which it had initially aspired.

The enemies of the S.S. and the writers of the abundant literature which concentrated later on its more notorious misdeeds presented it as a State within the Reich, if not as the very Reich itself. This is an exaggerated view. Even after 20th July 1944, the S.S. was far from representing the supreme might which some are so fond of describing. Its power stopped before the other fortresses of the regime – the Party headed by Bormann, the propaganda machine operated by Goebbels and the Wehrmacht.

Himmler's signature, natural size.

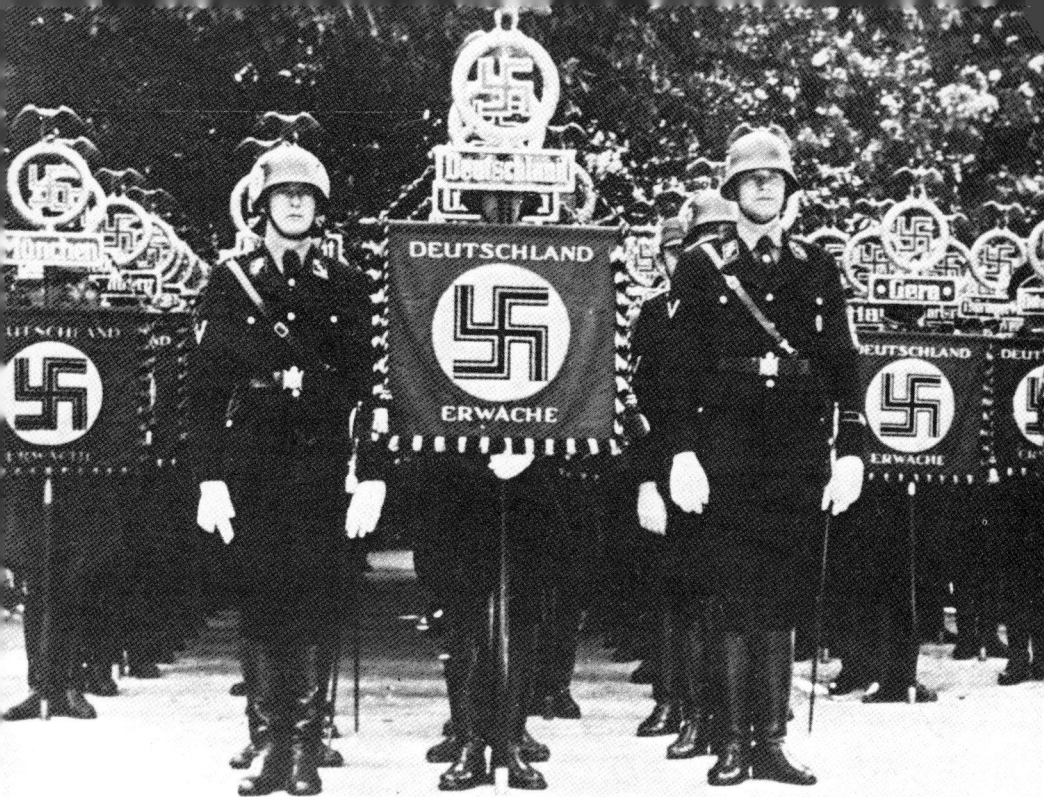

In its repressive tasks, the S.S. was to lose the character of the new aristocracy which Himmler claimed for it.

The powerful Gestapo and the ubiquitous S.D. were constrained to beat a retreat before their rivals. The S.S. was now far from possessing the power of the Ogpu in Russia. Already in 1943, Bormann had notified Himmler that the S.D. was forbidden to supervise Party matters. The ten general commissars for the Eastern occupational zone completely failed to acknowledge the authority of the *Reichsführer S.S.* The Gauleiters scoffed at his representatives.

Himmler's authority eventually came to be opposed in that part of the Black Order that he had cherished above all others and for which he held the highest hopes, the Waffen S.S. This organisation gradually became a stranger to the S.S. Fashioned by a long and terrible war, swollen and transformed by the constant inclusion of foreign soldiers of all nationalities, it was no longer recognisable except in its own leaders. Gradually, it became a body apart from the Order which had brought it to birth to fashion a new phenomenon. In its wild despair and its lucid nihilism, the Waffen S.S. recalled the volunteer corps of 1919 and 1920, who fought only for their black flags and their comrades.

APPENDIX I

BADGES OF RANK OF THE ALLGEMEINE S.S. (1934)

1. *On the collar*

These badges were worn on the left of the collar up to and including the rank of Obersturmbannführer. They were worn on both sides of the collar from the rank of Standartenführer upwards.

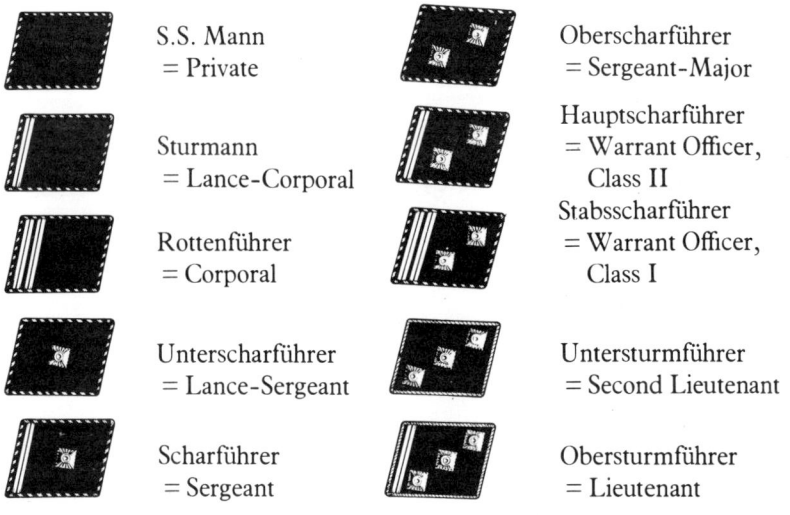

S.S. Mann = Private

Sturmann = Lance-Corporal

Rottenführer = Corporal

Unterscharführer = Lance-Sergeant

Scharführer = Sergeant

Oberscharführer = Sergeant-Major

Hauptscharführer = Warrant Officer, Class II

Stabsscharführer = Warrant Officer, Class I

Untersturmführer = Second Lieutenant

Obersturmführer = Lieutenant

 Hauptsturmführer = Captain

 Brigadeführer = Brigadier

 Sturmbannführer = Major

 Gruppenführer = Major-General

 Obersturmbannführer = Lieutenant-Colonel

 Obergruppenführer = Lieutenant-General

 Standartenführer = Colonel

 Reichsführer S.S. = (no equivalent)

 Oberführer = (no equivalent)

2. *Epaulettes*

 From Untersturmführer to Hauptsturmführer

 From Sturmbannführer to Standartenführer

 From S.S. Mann to Stabsscharführer

 From Oberführer to Obergruppenführer

 Reichsführer S.S.

3. *Seniority Badges*

These chevrons must not be confused with those of the Waffen S.S. They were worn on the upper part of the right arm.

 Members of the S.S. or the Party who joined up before 30th January 1933. Aluminium thread ribbon with black bands on a black ground.

 Former members of the police, the Reichswehr, the S.A. or the N.S.K.K.

 Former members of the Stahlhelm.

APPENDIX II

BADGES AND DECORATIONS OF THE ALLGEMEINE S.S. AND THE WAFFEN S.S.

Official armband of the S.S. Red with two black stripes. White disc and black swastika.

Armband of the S.S. members of the Reichstag (*Reichstagsabgeordnete*). It was the official armband, decorated with two gilt stripes.

S.S. eagle, worn from 1936 onwards on the left arm instead of the armband on the grey-green battledress.

Silver-plated badge, worn on the chest of the dress uniform.

Civil badge of the S.S. Black and silver.

Silver-plated ski instructor's badge, common to S.S. and S.A. (1933).

Silver-plated and black pilot's badge, common to the S.S. and S.A. (1931 to 1933).

Badge of sporting attainments of the Germanic S.S. (1943). Two categories: bronze and silver. The *Sieg* runes were in black enamel. Worn on the left breast pocket.

Medal in recognition of 25 years of service in the S.S. (years before 1933 counted double). Gilt swastika with, on the reverse, the inscription: FÜR TREUE DIENSTE IN DER S.S. (for faithful service in the S.S.). Blue ribbon with gilt Sieg runes.

 Medal in recognition of 12 years' service. Silver-plated medal and Sieg runes. Same inscription.

 Medal in recognition of 8 or 4 years' service. Colour bronze. Figure 8 or 4 on the reverse.

 *Bandenkampfabzeichen* (insignia of the war against the partisans), instituted by Hitler on 30th January 1944. Bronze for 20 days combat, silver for 50 days and gold for more than 100.

 Death's Head on peaked cap (1929 to 1936). White aluminium.

 Death's Head on peaked cap (after 1936). White aluminium.

 *Forage* cap Death's Head (from 1934 onwards). White aluminium.

Eagle on peaked cap (1929 to 1936). White aluminium.

Eagle on peaked cap (after 1936). White aluminium.

Eagle worn on left of forage cap (1934 to 1938). White aluminium on black fabric ground.

Eagle on left of forage cap (from 1938 onwards).

Helmet badges of the Standarten of the Allgemeine S.S. On the right are the black runes on a white field. To the left of the helmet is the red escutcheon with a black swastika.

First and second versions of the helmet badges of the Liebstandarte. The left hand escutcheon is in black, white and red.

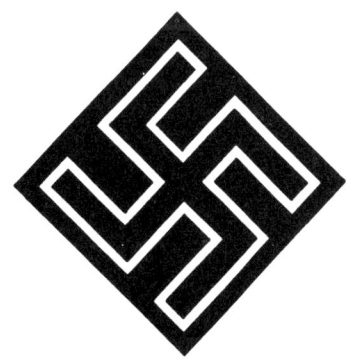 

Helmet badge of the S.S-V.T. Black and white.

APPENDIX III

SPECIAL BADGES OF THE ALLGEMEINE S.S.

1. *Arm badges*

These badges, woven in silver thread on a black ground, were worn on the left sleeve of the uniform jacket. They could also be worn on the left of the collar, along with the number of the unit.

S.S.-H.A. (S.S. Hauptamt = S.S. Central Office)

Medical service

S.S. courts and legal services

Rusha (Service of Race and Population)

S.D. (Security Service)

Cavalry Units

Pioneers

Alpine Units

Motorised Units

Band

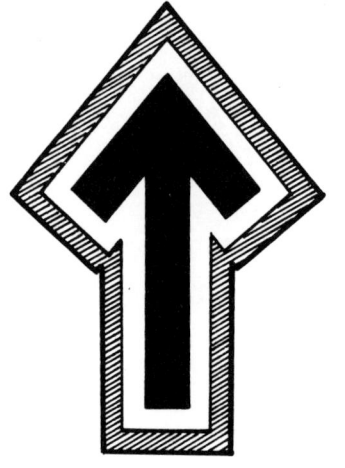

Badge worn by former pupils of the Reichsführerschulen. Tyr rune, the symbol of loyalty. Black on white ground, surrounded with red. Woven. Worn on the left shoulder.

Collar badge of Hitler's aide-de-camp. Eif rune (black ground, silver-plated rune).

APPENDIX IV

ARMBANDS

The armbands worn on the left indicated membership of a major department, an S.S. Oberabschnitt (District) or a unit.

Reichsführer S.S.'s personal Staff. Above, early model. Below, later model.

S.S. Hauptamt (S.S. Central Office), early and later models.

S.D. (Security Service) – worn by Senior Officers.

Rusha (Service of Race and Population) – worn by Senior Officers.

Four examples of armbands of S.S. Oberabschnitte (Districts).

South West
Central
Rhine
Elbe

Four examples of Standarten (Units) of the Allgemeine S.S.

Armband of S.S. Ehrenführer (Member of Honour of the S.S.) Ivory-coloured with aluminium thread embroidery.

Four armbands of S.S. senior officers, embroidered in aluminium thread with black bands. From top to bottom: Amtchef (Executive), Hauptabteilungsleiter (Head of Principal Department), Abteilungsleiter (Head of Department) and Referent (Consultant) on the General Staff of the R.F. S.S. (Reichsführer S.S.).

APPENDIX V

TERRITORIAL ORGANISATION OF THE S.S. (1943)

The territory of the Greater German Reich was divided into nineteen *S.S.-Oberabschnitte* (Districts), to which four were added from the occupied territories. Each of these regions was put under the authority of a *Höherer S.S.-und-Polizeiführer*, who had all police powers within his territory, representing the *Reichsführer S.S.* with a delegated authority in the name of the S.S. Only the Waffen S.S. generals demurred at coming under his authority. He was assisted by a *Stabsführer der Allgemeinen S.S.* (Allgemeine S.S. General Staff), covering several departments: the *Allgemeine S.S.* (which became ever weaker during the War), the S.D., *Rusha*, etc. The police units which did not depend on the Waffen S.S. and the special commands for security operations came under the direct orders of the *Höherer S.S.-und-Polizeiführer*.

List of S.S. Oberabschnitte:

1. Donau = Danube
2. Alpenland = Alps
3. Süd = South
4. Westmark = West March
5. Südwest = South West
6. Rhein = Rhine

7.	West	= West
8.	Nordsee	= North Sea
9.	Weichsel	= Vistula
10.	Nordost	= North East
11.	Warthe	= Warthe
12.	Südost	= South East
13.	Böhmen-Mähren	= Bohemia/Moravia
14.	Elbe	= Elba
15.	Main	= Main
16.	Fulda-Werra	= Fulda-Werra
17.	Mitte	= Central
18.	Spree	= Spree
19.	Ostsee	= Baltic Sea

to which the following four were added in the occupied territories:

1.	Nordwest	= North West (Hoiland)
2.	Nord	= North (Norway)
3.	Ukraine	= Ukraine (South West Russia)
4.	Ostland	= East (West Russia)

APPENDIX VI

MAIN EVENTS IN THE HISTORY OF THE S.S.

7th October	1900	Birth of Heinrich Himmler.
9th November	1919	Revolution in Germany. The Republic is proclaimed.
1st January	1920	Hitler joins the D.A.P.
29th June	1921	Hitler becomes Chairman of the N.S.D.A.P.
2nd August	1921	Captain Röhm founds the S.A.
1st March	1923	Hitler sets up the Stabswache (Bodyguard), two months later to become the Stosstruppe Hitler (Hitler Stormtroops).
27th August	1923	Himmler joins the N.S.D.A.P.
9th November	1923	Munich Putsch. Flag of Blood.
12th March	1925	Himmler is introduced to Hitler.
9th November	1925	The Stosstruppe Hitler becomes the Schutzstaffel (S.S. = Defence Squadron).
4th July	1926	Hitler hands over the Flag of Blood into S.S. keeping.
6th January	1929	Himmler appointed Reichsführer S.S. (280 men), subject to the S.A.
5th January	1931	Röhm reorganises the S.A.

243

2nd April	1931	S.A. Putsch at Berlin (Stennes) carried out by the S.S. (Daluege).
14th June	1931	Reinhard Heydrich is introduced to Himmler.
5th October	1931	Establishment of the S.D. (Security Service) under Heydrich.
31st December	1931	Himmler issues his Orders governing the marriage of members of the S.S.
25th January	1932	Himmler appointed as Security Head of the Brown House.
30th January	1933	Hitler becomes Chancellor of the Reich.
28th February	1933	The Reichstag Fire. A Decree for the Protection of the People and the State. The S.A. and the S.S. are allowed to make arrests and internments of political enemies.
28th February	1933	Setting up of Politische Bereitschaften S.S. (standing armed detachments) in the regions of Germany.
5th March	1933	Establishment of the concentration camp at Dachau, supervised by the S.S. Totenkopf.
9th March	1933	Himmler appointed Prefect of Police at Munich.
17th March	1933	Sepp Dietrich sets up the S.S. Stabswache. It replaces the Reichswehr in mounting guard before the Chancellery.
27th April	1933	Goering sets up the Gestapo in Prussia.
1st September	1933	The S.S. Stabswache becomes the Leibstandarte S.S. Adolf Hitler.
10th April	1934	Himmler appointed Head of Gestapo.
20th June	1934	Th. Eike appointed as Head of the S.S. Totenkopfverbände and Inspector of the Concentration Camps.
30th June	1934	The Night of the Long Knives. The executions were carried out by the Leibstandarte and the Totenkopf-verbände. Heydrich appointed Gruppen-führer S.S.

2nd July	1934	Schellenberg joins the S.D.
20th July	1934	The S.S. becomes independent of the S.A., with a strength of 200,000 men.
25th July	1934	Assassination of Chancellor Dollfuss at Vienna.
24th September	1934	Himmler sets up the S.S. Verfüngungstruppe.
1st November	1934	The Reichswehr authorises the setting up of two S.S. Officers' Schools, the Junkerschulen.
7th November	1934	The S.S. Central Office is set up in Berlin.
6th March	1935	The first number of the Schwarzes Korps (the S.S. magazine) appears.
16th March	1935	Hitler brings back compulsory military service. Establishment of the Wehrmacht. The S.S. Verfügungstruppen are made official.
30th June	1935	Himmler inaugurates the S.S. Junkerschule of Brunswick, controlled by Hausser.
15th September	1935	Nuremberg Congress. Racial laws.
17th June	1936	Himmler Head of all police forces. Heydrich takes over control of the Sipo and Daluege the Orpo.
1st October	1936	Paul Hausser appointed Brigadeführer and Inspector of the S.S. Verfügungstruppen.
9th November	1936	Establishment of the S.S. Persönlicher Stab Reichsführer S.S. (Himmler's personal General Staff).
4th February	1938	Resignation of Generals Blomberg and Fritsch. Hitler Supreme Commander.
11th March	1938	The Anschluss. The S.S. Leibstandarte is first to enter Vienna.
17th August	1938	Decree by Hitler apportioning the military responsibilities of the Wehrmacht and the S.S., respectively.
29th September	1938	Germany officially takes over the Sudetenland. The S.S. Verfügungstruppe is placed under the Wehrmacht's command in case of conflict.

15th March	1939	Occupation of Bohemia. Himmler in Prague.
1st September	1939	Polish Campaign. Baptism of fire. Heavy losses. Action by the first Einsatzkommandos.
27th September	1939	Establishment of the Waffen S.S. and the R.S.H.A. (National Security Central Office).
2nd March	1940	The title "Waffen S.S." made official.
1st April	1940	Gruppenführer Berger appointed Head of the S.S. Hauptamt (S.S. Central Office, responsible for recruitment).
20th April	1940	Establishment of the Nordland Regiment with Danish and Norwegian volunteers.
25th May	1940	Establishment of the Westland Regiment with Flemish volunteers.
May–June	1940	Campaign in the West (Leibstandarte, Totenkopf, Polizeidivision, Verfügungsdivision).
1st August	1940	Establishment of the S.S. Führungshauptamt (High Command of the Waffen S.S.), under Brigadeführer Hans Jüttner.
13th March	1941	Keitel's Directive. Himmler put in charge of special political and police functions in the East.
1st April	1941	Official establishment of the Wiking Division (Steiner) with Flemish and Scandinavian volunteers.
6th April	1941	German troops enter Yugoslavia, headed by "Das Reich", commanded by Hausser. Leibstandarte in Greece.
10th May	1941	Official establishment of the Einsatzgruppen for the suppression of opposition and performance of security functions in the rear of the Eastern Front.
22nd June	1941	Operation Barbarossa (Das Reich, Leibstandarte, Totenkopf and S.S. Polizei).
27th September	1941	Heydrich appointed Protector of Bohemia/Moravia.

7th December	1941	The Nacht und Nebel (Night and Mist) Order of the O.K.W. (Oberkommando der Wehrmacht – Wehrmacht High Command) concerning the deportation of dangerous inhabitants of the occupied countries.
20th January	1942	Wannsee Conference on the Final Solution.
16th February	1942	Himmler orders the destruction of the Warsaw Ghetto.
3rd March	1942	Gruppenführer Oswald Pohl appointed Head of the W.V.H.A. (Central Office of the Administration and Economy) to supervise the concentration camps for economic purposes from 30th April onwards.
4th June	1942	Assassination of Heydrich.
17th July	1942	Himmler made responsible for security in the occupied territories of the West.
31st January	1943	Kaltenbrunner becomes Head of the R.S.H.A. (National Security Central Office).
March	1943	The Waffen S.S. is opened to non-Germanic European peoples (Ukrainians, Estonians, Latvians).
15th March	1943	Kharkov re-taken by the Panzerkorps S.S. under Hausser.
22nd July	1943	Laval authorises Frenchmen to enlist in the S.S. Skorzeny frees Mussolini.
October	1943	Seven élite divisions of the Waffen S.S. become the S.S. Panderdivisionen (S.S. Tank Divisions).
15th November	1943	The Leibstandarte breaks the Soviet offensive in the Kiev sector.
17th February	1944	The Wiking and the Wallonie Legions at Cherkasy.
June–August	1944	The S.S., Hitlerjugend, Das Reich, Götz von Berlichingen, Hohenstaufen and Freundsberg Divisions in Normandy to oppose the Allied disembarkation.
20th July	1944	Attempt on Hitler's life.

21st July	1944	Himmler becomes Commander in Chief of the Army of the Interior.
3rd August	1944	Himmler's speech on the European S.S.
25th September	1944	The Ninth and Tenth S.S. Divisions at Arnhem.
2nd October	1944	End of the Warsaw Rising.
16th December	1944	The Ardennes Offensive. Three S.S. divisions besieged at Budapest by the Red Army.
20th January	1945	Himmler Commander in Chief of the Armies of the Vistula.
6th March	1945	Final German counter-offensive in Hungary under the orders of Sepp Dietrich.
2nd May	1945	Berlin, defended by the foreign volunteers of the Waffen S.S., capitulates.
8th May	1945	Capitulation of Germany.
24th May	1945	Suicide of Himmler at the age of 44.

APPENDIX VII

STRUCTURE OF THE S.S.

Ahnenerbe: An ideological, intellectual and cultural research organisation within the S.S.

Allgemeine S.S.: The General S.S. It was gradually to disappear after the taking of power and with the onset of War, in favour of specialist organisations set up or controlled by the S.S.

Einsatzgruppen: Special units dependent on the S.D. and responsible for repressive measures behind the front line.

Führungshauptamt (S.S.-F.H.A.): The supreme body of the Waffen S.S., responsible for the instruction, supplies and organisation of units in the field.

Gestapo (Geheime Staatspolizei): The secret State police for political purposes; it was only one of the active departments of the R.S.H.A.

S.S.-Hauptamt (S.S.-H.A.): The central office of the S.S., responsible for general administration, particularly recruitment, personnel and the ideological training of the Waffen S.S.

Höherer S.S.-und-Polizeiführer (H.S.S.P.F.): A high-ranking official, responsible for the control of the police and the co-ordination of S.S. activities, representing Himmler in every military region and in certain occupied territories.

Lebensborn: An organisation to ensure social and medical aid to young mothers and illegitimate children of S.S. couples.

Napola (Nationalpolitische Erzeihungsanstalten): Training colleges for future executives of the Reich.

Ordensburg: Schools for Party executives, not directly dependent on the S.S.

Orpo (Ordnungspolizei): All police forces in uniform.

R.K.F. (Reichskommissariat für die Festigung deutschen Volksturms: Commissariat for Germanic expansion in Eastern Europe.

R.S.H.A. (Reichssicherheitshauptamt): Overall responsibility for the security, information and police services of the Reich.

Rusha (Rasse-und Siedlungshauptamt): Responsible for implementation of the racial policy and for German colonisation in the East.

S.D. (Sicherheitsdienst): Information, espionage and security service of the S.S. Its competence and powers were extremely extensive.

Sipo (Sicherheitspolizei): Security police on which the Gestapo (the political police) and the Kripo (criminal police) depended.

Sonderkommando: Unit acting under special instructions.

Totenkopfwachsturmbanne: Death's Head units responsible for guarding the concentration camps; they replaced the Totenkopfverbände in 1939.

Verfügungstruppen (S.S.-V.T.): Militarised S.S. units, set up in 1934, from which the later Waffen S.S. emerged.

Vomi (Volksdeutsche Mittelstelle): The department responsible for Germans abroad.

Waffen S.S.: Armed forces dependent on the S.S. for recruitment, instruction, subsistence, administration and promotion, but coming under the O.K.H. (Oberkommando des Heeres, the High Command of the Land Army) and the O.K.W. (Oberkommando der Wehrmacht, the High Command of the Armed Forces) in the conduct of operations.

W.V.H.A. (Wirtschaftsverwaltungshauptamt): The central economic office of the S.S. responsible, among other duties, for the administration of the concentration camps.

PHOTOGRAPHY

The illustrations in the present volume come from private collections, photographic agencies, the *Bundesarchiv* at Koblenz, the *Weltkriegsbücherei* at Stuttgart, the *Ullstein Bilderdienst* at Berlin and the *Institut für Zeitgeschichte* at Vienna. We should like to thank all those who have helped to collect this documentary material.

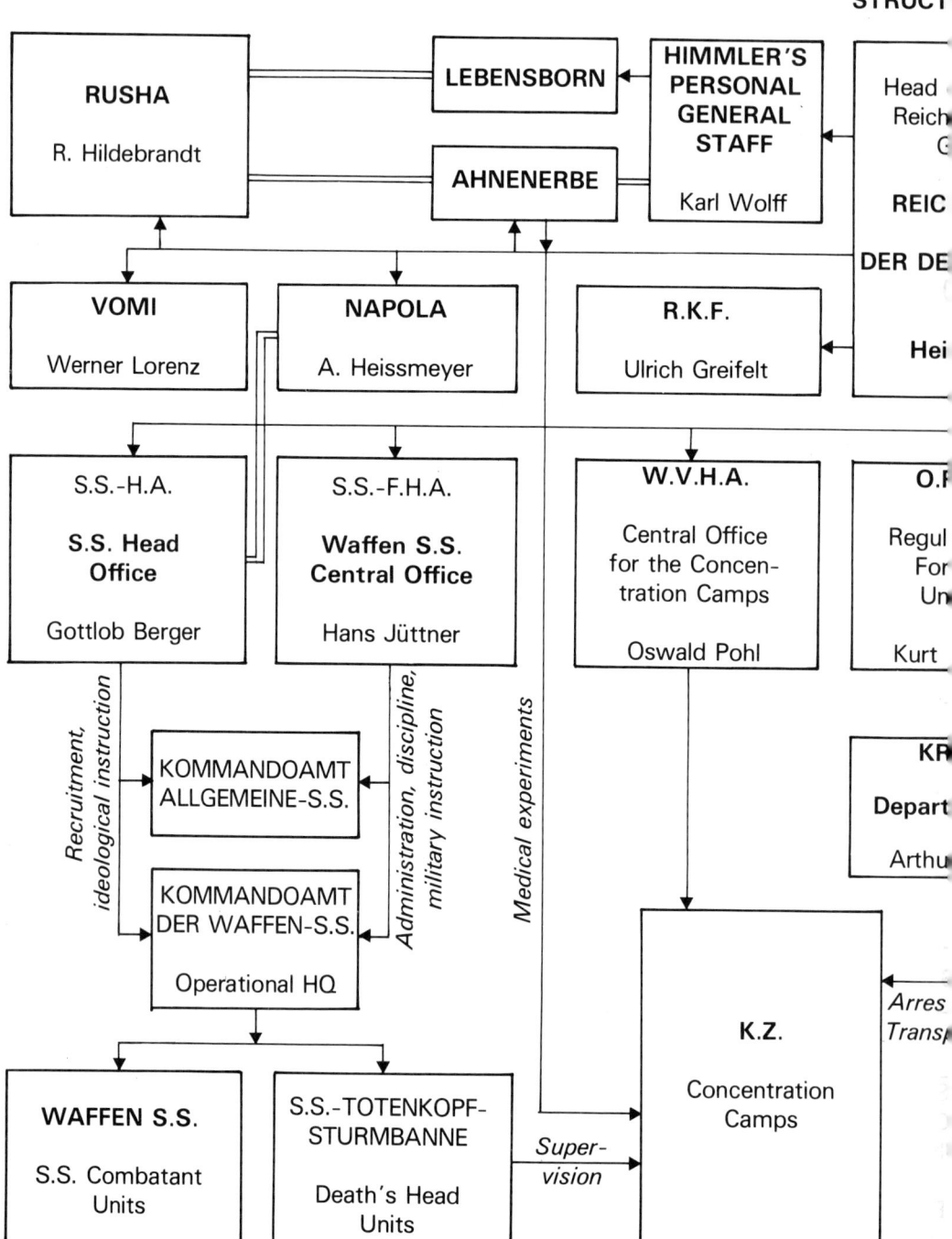

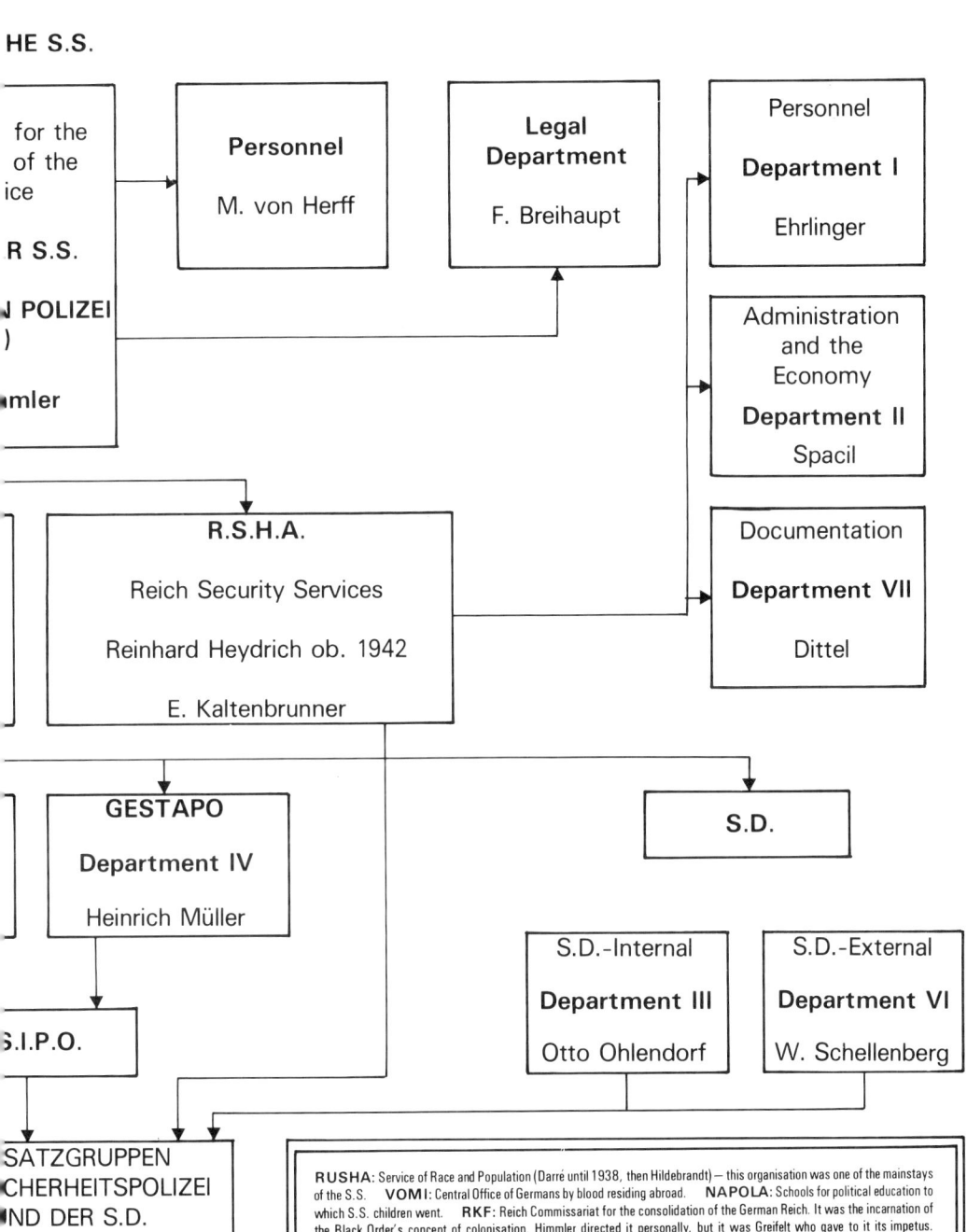

INDEX

Page numbers in italic refer to illustrations

Adenauer, Konrad 20
Ahnenerbe 185–99, *185–6, 198*, 202–4, 249, 252
Ahnenpass 141
Albert of Brandenberg *131*
Allgemeine S.S. 80, 81, 249
Alphabet, runic 195
Alquen, Gunther d' *105*
Archaeological excavations 194, *194*, 195, 200
Ares and Aphrodite *191*
Armaments industry 98, 199
Austria 112–14, *114*
Austrian Legion *113*

Baltikum Volunteer Corps 14, 18, *19, 20*, 21, 23, *23*, 27, *28*
Baptism in the S.S. 154
Beger, (Prof.) 197
Berchtold, Josef (Lieut.) 32, 34, 42, 45, *46*
Berger, Gottlob 99
Best, Werner (Dr) 109–10, *109*
Black Corps *102*, 104–5, 134–5, 155, 175
Blutfahne (Flag of Blood) 34, *38*, 44, 129, 130, 208
Bolshevism, 93
Book of Ancestors 141
Brecker, Arno: *Strength 207*
Brunswick Hussars *43*

Chamberlain, Houston *53*

Chemnitz 42
Children and Youth 149–54, *169–70*, *173–4*, 177–8
Communism, 83–4, 86, 93
Concentration Camp *see* Konzentrationslager
Crime and punishment 215
Currency: devaluation *33*
Czechoslovakia 115–7, *116*

Daluege, Kurt *63*, 107
Danzig demonstration *119*
Darre, Walter (Dr) 142, *143*, 187, *187*
Deutsche Arbeiterpartei 23
Deutsche Heimatfront 115
Deutsche Wirtschaftsbetriebe (D.W.B.) 97
Deutsches Ahnenerbe, see Ahnenerbe
Diehls, Rudolph 71
Dietrich, Sepp 33, 70, *81*
Dirlewanger Brigade *121*
Drexler, Anton 23

Eckart, Dietrich 24
Ehrhardt, (Capt.) 28
Ehrhardt Brigade *31*
Eichmann, Adolf (Lieut-Col.) 123, *123*, 124
Eike, Theodor (Brig.) 73, 74
Einsatzgruppen 249
"Enemies of the regime" 106

Feder, Gottfried 24
Frank, Karl Hermann 117
Freemasonry 218
Freundekreis Heinrich Himmler 102–3
Frick, Wilhelm (Dr) 71
Frontbann 39

Galke, Bruno 188, 190
Geheime Staatspolizei (Gestapo) 70, 105, *106*, 108, 249
German Homeland Front 115
German Workers' Party 23
Germany
  "A vision of the future" 27
  Map *12, 13*
  Revolution 16, *17*
Gestapo 70, 105, *106*, 108, 249, 253
Gobineau Josef de *53*
Goering, Hermann (Capt.) 30, *30*, 62, 70, 125
Graf, Ulrich, 33, 34
"Grand Inquisitor and his Shadow" *91*
Grese, Irma *219*

Haganah 123
Harrer, Karl 24
Haselunne Convent 175
Haupt, Joachim 171
Hausser, Paul (Gen.) 100
Heiden, Erhard 45, *47*
Heissmayer, (Lieut-Gen.) 174

254

Henlein, (Dr) 115
Henry the First, the Fowler 133, *133*
Heydrich, Reinhard Tristan 65, 66, *66*, 107, *112*, *120*, *217*
Hildebrandt, Richard 143
Himmler, Gundrund *147*
Himmler, Heinrich 35, *35*, 47–50, 52–8, *54*, *59*, 66, *71*, 73, *74*, 75, 78, *87*, *90*, *103*, 107, *107*, 117, 122, 133, 145, 150, 151, 153–4, 187, 192, *198*, 199, 205–26, *214*, *222*, *224*, *225*
Hirt, (Prof.) 196–7 *197*
Hitler, Adolf 21–5, *22*, 33, 36, 39, 42, *45*–6, *49*, 62, *62*, 63, 69, 75, *81*, *101*, 102, *115*, *118*, 128, *159*, 172, 174
Hoffman, Heinrich *46*
Hofmann, Otto 143
Hohne, Rolf 195
Holst, (Dr) *203*
Huber *107*

Imperial Hussars *43*

Jankuhn, Herbert 195–6
Jews 25, 28, *50*, 91, 117, 120, 122–7, 217, *218*
Jost, Heinz *110*
Julfest 155–6, 177

Kaltenbrunner, Ernst *111*
Kaminsky, Bronislav *122*
Kammler (Engineer) 98
Kempka (Maj.) *214*
Keppler, Wilhelm 102
Kern, Erwin (Lieut.) *22*
Konigsplatz, Munich *210*
Konzentrationslager (K.Z.) 72, 73, 83, *85*–7,

86–8, 96–7, *98*, 119, *124*, 126, 127, 197, 199, *203*, *216*, 218, 252
Kranefuss, Fritz 103
Kriebel, Hermann 30
Kripo 108
Krohn, Friedrich 24

Landsberg Prison *49*
Lebensborn 147, 148–9, 249, 252
Lutze, Victor *87*

Madagascar 124
Marienburg Castle *132*
Marriage 153, 200–1
Matthausen Quarries *98*
Maurice, Emile 33
Mayr, (Capt.) 26
Muller, Heinrich *107*, *109*

Napola 157, 159, 161–5, *162*, *164*–5, 167–9, 171–2, 174–5, 177, 184, *184*, 250, 252
National Security Central Office 108–111
National Socialist German Workers Party *see Nazional-Sozialistiche Deutsche Arbeiter Partei*
Naujocks, Alfred *112*
Naumann, Erich *126*
Nazional-Sozialistiche Deutsche Arbeiter Partei 27, 29, 34, *37*, *54*, *59*
Nebe *107*
"Night of the Long Knives" 76, *76*, 77, *77*
Nordic Civilisation *188*–9
Norkus, Herbert 177–8
Noske 20
Nuremberg Congress, 1934 *211*

Nuremberg Congress, 1935 *213*

Oberland Volunteer Corp *36*
Odal Rune *141*
Ohlendorf, Otto (Brig.) *110*, 127, 139–40, *140*
Olympic Stadium, Berlin *196*
"One People, One Reich, One Fuhrer" *92*
Ordensburgen *160*–*1*
Orgesh 27

Pohl, Oswald (Lieut-Gen.) 96–7, *97*, 126, 190
Poland *120*, 123–4

Rascher, Sigmund 197, 199
Reichskriegsflagge (Reich Flag of War) 35, 49
Reichssicherheitshaupttampt (R.H.S.A.) 108–11, 250, 253
Reichswehr 99
Religion 175, *176*
Rohm, Ernst (Capt.) 26, 28, 39, *59*, 62, *62*, 69
Rosenberg, Alfred *193*
Rosenwinck, Alois 42
Rossbach *Freikorps* 29
Rossbach, Gerhard *29*
Rusha *141*–2, *142*, 144, 153, 250, 252
Russkaya Osvoboditelnaya Narodnya Armiya 122
Rust, Bernhard (Dr) 157

Schafer, Ernst 197
Schellenbaum (Belltree) *209*
Schellenberg, Walter 108, *108*
Schlagter, Albert 179–80
Schleif, Hans (Dr) 195
Schreck, Julius *32*, 41–2
Schultz, Paul 63

Schutzpolizei 73
Schutzstaffel 40
Schwarze Totenkopfhusaren
 43
Schwarzes Korps 102,
 104–5, 134–5, 155,
 175
Security Police 107, 108
Seyss-Inquart, (Dr) 115
Sicherheitsdienst (S.D.) 67,
 88, 89, 90, 105, 112,
 218
 Einsatzgruppen 120,
 120, 124–5, 127, 220
Sicherheitspolizei 107, 108
Sievers, Wolfram 190–2
Socialist Party 10, 11
Solstice celebrations
 180–182, 181
Sonderkommandos 72, 77
S.S. 15, 40–2, 44–7, 51,
 53–9, 56, 60, 64, 64,
 67, 69, 71, 77–9,
 81–3, 82, 94–7, 96,
 102, 104, 128, 131,
 133, 135, 136, 137,
 138–9, 140–1,
 144–6, 149, 171,
 195, 205, 206,
 208–15, 216, 221–2,
 223, 224–5, 226,
 250, 252, 253
 Ehrenfuhrer 104
 Fordernde Mitgleider 102
 Members, 1925 40
 Politische Bereitschaften
 (Political Reserves) 73
 Reichsfuhrer 48
 Untergruppe 65
S.S. *Hilferinnen* 148, 150
S.S. *Leibstandarte Adolf*
 Hitler 70, 70, 79, 81,
 117, 137

S.S. Special Commando Unit
 see Sonderkommandos
S.S. *Standarte* 89 113
Stabswache (Bodyguard) 31
Stadingen 201
Stennes, Walther 61, 63
Steinbach, Edgar 42, 183
Steiner, Felix (Maj.) 100
Stosstruppe Adolf Hitler 31,
 32, 40
Strasser, Otto 77
Strassor, Gregor 49
Strosstruppen 28
Sturmabteilung (S.A.) 27,
 29, 31, 34, 39, 46,
 59, 61, 67, 69, 71,
 75, 76
Sturmstaffel 40
Sudeten German Volunteer
 Corps 115–6, 117
Sudetendeutsche Partei 115
Swastika 26, 28, 190

Teutonic Knights, Order of
 the 130–2
Thule Society 23, 26
Totenkopfverbande 73, 84

Ultramontanes 89
U.S.S.R. 124

Verfugungstruppe (Waffen
 S.S.) 100, 102, 226,
 250
 Germania Regiment 99
Vogler, Eugen (Dr) 103
Volkischer Beobachter 45
Volunteer Corps 57
Vomi 250, 252

von Blomberg, (Marshal)
 100, 101
von Braun, Wernher 98
von Eberstein, Freidrich
 Karl 66
von Fritsch, (Gen.) 101,
 101
von Hindenburg, (Marshal)
 69
von Kahr, (P.M.) 77
von Kluwer, (Lieut-Col.) 17
von Mildenstein, Leonard
 122
von Osten, Lina 66
von Salomon, Franz Pfeffer
 44, 45, 59, 62
von Salza, Hermann 130

Waffen S.S. *see*
 Verfugungstruppe
Wagner, Gauleiter 208
Wagner, Richard 51
War, 1914–18
 Europe: Pre-war 9
 Germany: Pre-war 10
 Peace Treaty 8
Weber, Christian 33
Weiss, Bernhard 50
Weltanschauung 51
Wehrmacht *see Reichswehr*
Wewelsburg Castle 134,
 135
Windsor, (Duke of) 99
Wirth, Hermann 186, 188
Wolf, Karl 154
Women 146–7, 148, 151
Wust, Walter 188, 190–2

Zeppelin Field, Nuremberg
 (statue) 207